Financial Exclusion

Palgrave Macmillan Studies in Banking and Financial Institutions

Series Editor: **Professor Philip Molyneux**

The Palgrave Macmillan Studies in Banking and Financial Institutions will be international in orientation and include studies of banking within particular countries or regions, and studies of particular themes such as Corporate Banking, Risk Management, Mergers and Acquisitions, etc. The books will be focused upon research and practice, and include up-to-date and innovative studies on contemporary topics in banking that will have global impact and influence.

Titles include:

Santiago Carbó, Edward P.M. Gardener and Philip Molyneux
FINANCIAL EXCLUSION

Munawar Iqbal and Philip Molyneux
THIRTY YEARS OF ISLAMIC BANKING
History, Performance and Prospects

Philip Molyneux and Munawar Iqbal
BANKING AND FINANCIAL SYSTEMS IN THE ARAB WORLD

Palgrave Macmillan Studies in Banking and Financial Institutions
Series Standing Order ISBN 1–4039–4872–0

You can receive future titles in this series as they are published by placing a standing order. Please contact your bookseller or, in case of difficulty, write to us at the address below with your name and address, the title of the series and one of the ISBNs quoted above.

Customer Services Department, Macmillan Distribution Ltd, Houndmills, Basingstoke, Hampshire, RG21 6XS, England

Financial Exclusion

By Santiago Carbó, Edward P.M. Gardener and
Philip Molyneux

First published 2005 by
PALGRAVE MACMILLAN
Houndmills, Basingstoke, Hampshire RG21 6XS and
175 Fifth Avenue, New York, N.Y. 10010
Companies and representatives throughout the world

PALGRAVE MACMILLAN is the global academic imprint of the Palgrave Macmillan division of St. Martin's Press, LLC and of Palgrave Macmillan Ltd. Macmillan® is a registered trademark in the United States, United Kingdom and other countries. Palgrave is a registered trademark in the European Union and other countries.

ISBN-13: 978–1–4039–9051–8   hardback
ISBN-10: 1–4039–9051–4   hardback

This book is printed on paper suitable for recycling and made from fully managed and sustained forest sources.

A catalogue record for this book is available from the British Library.

Library of Congress Cataloging-in-Publication Data
Carbó, Santiago, 1966–
    Financial exclusion / by Santiago Carbó, Edward P.M. Gardener, and
    Philip Molyneux.
        p. cm. – (Palgrave Macmillan studies in banking and financial
    institutions)
    Includes bibliographical references and index.
    ISBN 1–4039–9051–4
        1. Financial services industry–Customer services. 2. Discrimination in
financial services. 3. Financial services industry–Government policy.
I. Gardener, Edward P.M. II. Molyneux, Philip. III. Title. IV. Series.

HG173.C28 2005
332.1′08–dc22   2004065452

10   9   8   7   6   5   4   3   2   1
14   13   12   11   10   09   08   07   06   05

Printed and bound in Great Britain by
Antony Rowe Ltd, Chippenham and Eastbourne

We dedicate this book to Professor Jack Revell who died in Cambridge on 4th November 2004. It is a small tribute to his foresight and contribution to the field of social banking and the respective role of proximity banking.

Contents

List of Tables

List of Figures

Glossary of Acronyms

ABCUL	Association of British Credit Unions Ltd
ABS	Asset-backed Security
AdFlag	AdFlag Adult Financial Literary Advisory Group
ACT	Automated Credit Transfer
APR	Annual Percentage Rate
ART	Aston Reinvestment Trust (UK)
ATM	Automated Teller Machine
BBA	British Bankers Association
BVA	Break-up Value Analysis
CABx	Citizen Advice Bureaux (UK)
CCA	Consumer Credit Act (1974 in the UK)
CCA	Consumer Credit Association (UK)
CCCS	Consumer Credit Counselling Service (UK)
CDFI	Community Development Financial Institution (UK)
CFI	Community Finance Initiative (UK)
CIS	Commonwealth of Independent States
CLFI	Community and Learning Finance Initiative (UK)
CRA	Community Reinvestment Act (US)
CRISIS	Centre for Research into Socially Inclusive Services (UK)
CRSP	Centre for Research into Social Policy
CSO	Central Services Organisation (for credit unions in the UK)
CU	Credit Union
DfES	Department for Education and Skills (UK)
DSS	Department of Social Security (UK)
DTI	Department of Trade and Industry
DETR	Department of the Environment, Transport and the Regions
EC	European Commission
ESRC	Economic and Social Research Council
ETA	Electronic Transfer Accounts (US)
EU	European Union
FDIC	Federal Deposit Insurance Corporation
FSA	Financial Services Authority (in the UK)
FSF	Financial Services Firm
GHS	General Household Survey (UK)

HBOS	Halifax Bank of Scotland
HMSO	Her Majesty's Stationery Office
HoH	Head of Household
HSBC	Hong Kong and Shanghai Banking Corporation
IDA	Individual Development Account (US)
IFAD	International Fund for Agricultural Development (Italy)
IFS	Institute of Financial Services (UK)
IMF	International Monetary Fund
IS	Income Support (UK)
IT	Information Technology
IWR	Insurance with Rent
JMLSG	Joint Money Laundering Steering Group (UK)
JSA	Job Seekers Allowance
KYC	Know Your Customer
LAPA	Lovian Anti Poverty Alliance (UK)
LDC	Lesser Developed Countries
LETS	Local Exchange Trading Schemes (UK)
LINK	LINK ATM Network (UK)
LTV	Life-Time-Value (of Customers)
MAT	Money Advice Trust (UK)
MPPI	Mortgage Payment Protection Insurance
NAW	National Assembly for Wales
NCC	National Consumer Council (UK)
NGO	Non Government Organisation
NPI	New Policy Institute (UK)
OECD	Organisation for Economic Co-operation and Development
OFT	Office of Fair Trading (UK)
PAT	Policy Action Teams (UK)
PC	Personal Computer
PFEG	Personal Finance Educational Group (UK)
PIU	Performance and Innovation Unit (UK)
PO	Post Office
POCA	Post Office Card Account (UK)
POCL	Post Office Counters Ltd
PSE	Poverty and Social Exclusion (UK)
PSHE	Personal, Social and Health Education (UK)
RAROC	Risk Adjusted Return on Capital
RBS	Royal Bank of Scotland
ROSCA	Rotating Savings and Credit Association
SBCS	Small Business Credit Scoring (US)
SBS	Small Business Service (UK)

SCF	Survey of Consumer Finances (US)
SEU	Social Exclusion Unit (UK)
SME	Small and Medium Size Enterprise
SSI	Supplementary Security Income (US)
SWM	Shareholder Wealth Maximisation
TSB	Trustee Savings Bank
VM	Value Maximisation
WEETU	Women's Employment Enterprise and Training Unit
WSBI	World Savings Banks Institute

Preface

This text examines contemporary issues relating to financial exclusion (the inability and/or reluctance of particular societal groups to access mainstream financial services) in Europe, US and the developing world. The text analyses access to finance and the role of government and financial institutions in promoting financial inclusion.

As the first book, as far as we are aware, to be written on the subject of financial exclusion we hope to make the following contributions:

- This book provides an evaluation of financial exclusion issues in Europe, US and the developing world;
- Provides analysis of the various public and private sector initiatives that have been introduced in Europe and the US to deal with financial exclusion;
- Discusses the role played by banks and other financial institutions aimed at attracting excluded clientele;
- Examines the role of government in dealing with financial exclusion which is becoming an important global policy issue;
- Offers an accessible text that will be of use to policymakers, financial institutions, consumer bodies, researchers and students of financial exclusion in both the developed and developing world.

This text could not have been completed without the help of various individuals and organisations. The authors wish to thank Fundacion de las Cajas de Ahorro Confederadas (FUNCAS) for their financial support on a research project on financial exclusion, parts of the contents and results of the project are included in the text. A special word of thanks also to Professor Ted Gardener's secretary, Gladys Humphreys, who valiantly typed and directed production of the initial proofs for this book.

Finally, thanks to all our families and loved ones for their usual forbearance with projects of this kind.

Edward P.M. Gardener and Philip Molyneux
Institute of European Finance
School for Business and Regional Development
University of Wales, Bangor
Gwynedd
Wales
LL57 2DG, UK

Santiago Carbó Valverde
Departamento de Teoria e Historia Economica
Facultad de CCEE y Empresariales
Campus Cartuja
Universidad de Granada
E-18071 – Granada
Spain

1
Introduction

This text is concerned with the increasingly important and problematic area of financial exclusion, broadly defined as the inability and/or reluctance of particular societal groups to access mainstream financial services. This has emerged as a major policy concern in the US and the UK. The case of these two countries is particularly interesting since these have the most strongly market-orientated financial systems in the world, and as such they provide a good 'laboratory' of the likely development path of financial exclusion, together with some possible policy solutions (by government, other interest groups and the financial services sector) in other deregulating financial sectors.

The accumulating evidence is that deregulation in financial sectors improves financial inclusion for some societal groups (more products become available to a bigger customer base), but may at the same time exacerbate it for others (for example, by emphasising greater customer segmentation and more emphasis on risk-based pricing and 'value added'). Concern with financial exclusion is also emerging in many European countries and a variety of different policy approaches are being developed. The issue of financial inclusion has also long been an issue throughout the developing world.

This text provides a broad comparative study of financial exclusion in the US, UK and other European countries. We also discuss issues relating to financial exclusion in developing countries. The aim is to explore the different paths of financial exclusion; assess the economic and other consequences of financial exclusion; consider the policy options that are being used and developed; and to produce an informed analysis of the possible strategic implications of financial exclusion for banks and other financial services firms

Aims and objectives

Research to date in the field of financial exclusion has been wide and diffuse. Much of it has been concerned with defining and documenting the nature, causes and consequences of financial exclusion, together with actual and proposed solutions: see, for example, Donovan and Palmer (1999), FSA (Financial Services Authority) (2000) and Sinclair (2001). Several specialist streams of research have emanated from this broad field. These include geographic and other 'space locations' (like social and economic) of financial exclusion: see Leyshon and Thrift (1995), Dymski and Li (2002) and Fuller and Jonas (2002); the role of bank strategies: see Alexander and Pollard (2000), Argent & Rolley (2000) and Boyce (2001); the future of mutuality: see Rossiter (1997) and Waite (2001); the genesis, evolution and efficiency of specialist financial institutions, like credit unions: see, for example, Fuller (1998), Hayton (2001) and McKillop *et al* (2002); and finance for small businesses in deprived communities: see Bank of England (2000 a & b). This is a select sample of a burgeoning literature, itself testimony to the growing incidence and policy importance of financial exclusion in modern, deregulating financial systems.

The present text has four main aims. First, it will compare the nature and contemporary context of financial exclusion in three important countries: the UK, US and Italy in the context of wider European experiences. The UK and the US are examples of strongly market-orientated financial systems where deregulation and the free market ethos in financial services have gone furthest. In both of these countries, financial exclusion has become a major policy concern. Italy and other European countries comprise another 'comparator' group of countries since (in contrast to the US and UK) financial services in many European system were highly regulated until the 1990s and they typically have bank-based systems where mutual banks (such as savings and cooperative banks) play a more important role in the provision of retail financial services. Financial exclusion appears to be emerging as a more significant policy concern in Italy and many other European countries, but this is not yet a widely documented and disseminated literature.

The second aim is to identify and evaluate the various policy options (both public and private) that are being developed in the various countries under study. Particular interest will be focused on the possible regulatory consequences for banks and other financial services firms.

The third aim will be to consider the strategic implications and possibilities for different types of banks. This will span both products and portfolio strategies that might be developed. Attention will be focused on whether social/political longer-term objectives are consistent with modern 'value maximisation' (VM) strategies.

The final aim is to outline financial exclusion issues in developing countries to see what can be learned (if anything) from policy issues undertaken in the US, UK and other developed systems.

The broad objective, then, is to provide a comprehensive, comparative survey of financial exclusion. This will provide some practical insight into the development path of financial exclusion, addressing it as both a problem and challenge, and related strategic implications for financial services firms in a modern deregulating financial system. The text should help to inform the thinking of banks' and other financial institutions' planners, strategists and policymakers.

A major part of this text relates to the compilation and dissemination of the burgeoning literature, both public and private. A very broad 'comparative model' will be used that will facilitate comparisons between the countries studied. This will also enable us to assess where possible the comparative success of different strategies pursued to date. Particular attention will be focused on the role of banks and other financial services firms.

2
Nature, Consequences and Policy Reactions: An Overview

Introduction

This chapter provides a broad overview of financial exclusion, with particular reference to UK and US experiences. It explores the meaning and various dimensions of financial exclusion. In addition, the chapter outlines various policy responses that have been used to tackle the problem of financial exclusion.

Nature and causes

Financial exclusion refers broadly to the inability (however occasioned) of some societal groups to access the financial system. At a policy level, it is part of the much wider concept of social exclusion and polarisation. Groups in society that are unable to access financial services are frequently unable to obtain other key social provision and financial exclusion can often exacerbate other kinds of social exclusion.

'Financial exclusion' is invariably experienced by poorer members of society. Significant numbers of low income people are apparently excluded from financial services spanning a range of basic products that include credit, insurance, bill-payment services and deposit account facilities. In the UK until recently around 1.5 million (7%) of households lacked any financial products at all and a further 4.4 million (20%) were on the margin of financial services, typically with little more than a bank account. Despite some improvement in recent years (BBA, 2002, pp. 4–6) financial exclusion remains a formidable challenge. Financial exclusion also appears to be concentrated both geographically and on certain groups of people.

A wider definition of financial exclusion is ... 'the inability to access necessary financial services in an appropriate form. Exclusion can come about as a result of problems with access, conditions, prices, marketing or self-exclusion in response to negative experiences or perceptions' (Sinclair, 2001). A number of aspects, or dimensions, of financial exclusion have been identified (FSA, 2000, p. 9):

- **access exclusion:** restricted access via the processes of risk assessment;
- **condition exclusion:** where the conditions attached to financial products make them unsuitable for the needs of some people;
- **price exclusion:** where some people can only access financial products at prices they cannot afford;
- **marketing exclusion:** where some people are effectively excluded by targeted marketing and sales;
- **self-exclusion:** people decide that there is no point in applying for a financial product because they believe that they would be refused. These beliefs can arise from many experiences and perceptions.

Together, these different kinds of financial exclusion comprise a complicated collection of barriers to entry to mainstream financial services for many societal groups.

Financial exclusion is currently of widespread interest in the UK – to government, the financial services industry and consumer groups. This is because of its implications and role in the wider issue of social exclusion. In the UK, the Labour government established the Social Exclusion Unit (SEU) soon after it assumed power in 1997. Both the Financial Services Authority (FSA) and the Bank of England have conducted major research and policy reviews of financial exclusion, and also focused on particular aspects (like small business finance).

One apparent cause of financial exclusion has been the growth of poverty. Between 1979 and 1994/5, for example, the real incomes of the poorest decile of the British population fell by eight per cent; average real incomes, though, rose significantly during this same period. During the 1980s and early 1990s, the income and wealth distribution in the UK became more unequal. A number of socio-economic factors have been important in this context, including incomes and income distribution, labour market changes, demographic trends, housing policy and tenure shifts, and welfare and financial reform (FSA, 2000, ch. 2).

It is a kind of paradox that the problem of financial exclusion has arisen from increased inclusion that has resulted in a small group of individuals and households being left behind. The intensity of trends like deregulation, globalisation and the concomitant rise of 'value maximisation' (VM) by banks appears also to be correlated positively with a growing incidence and awareness of financial exclusion. Boyce (2000), for example, shows that 'customer valuation' has become a means to increase shareholder income and wealth, almost invariably at the cost of further alienating the poor and disadvantaged.

The significant restructuring of the UK financial services industry in the 1980s and early 1990s contributed directly and indirectly to financial exclusion. The 1980s were characterised by an unprecedented growth in the UK financial services industry. Increased competition led to a continued search for new customers and greater customer segmentation. The 1990s recession, however, led to a 'flight to quality' by financial services firms. Expansion and increasing segmentation in financial services provision have both contributed to financial exclusion (FSA, 2000, p. 17).

Financial exclusion, then, appears to be the result of a complex, often interconnected set of factors. Socio-economic developments are clearly important. Concurrent developments in the financial services industry are also significant; financial exclusion has apparently been exacerbated by structural and strategic developments in the financial services industry. In particular, intensifying competition, the rise of 'customer value' concepts, increased customer segmentation and the pursuit of more affluent customers have been especially significant.

The financially excluded

The FSA in the UK report that outside the 'sharp end of financial exclusion' (i.e. around seven per cent of households in Britain do not have any mainstream financial products), many more individuals and households lack particular types of financial services. They quote recent research (FSA, 2000, p. 21) that includes the following statistics:

- between 15 per cent and 23 per cent of adults do not have a current (chequing) account;
- 31–37 per cent of households have no savings or investment products;
- 27 per cent of employees have no occupational or private pension;
- 45 per cent of households have no life insurance cover;
- 29 per cent have no access to credit from a mainstream provider.

Financial exclusion also appears to be concentrated on particular groups, like the following (Sinclair, 2001):

- the long-term unemployed;
- old-age pensioners;
- those excluded from earnings because of sickness or disability;
- female single parents;
- certain ethnic minority groups, especially Pakistani and Bangladeshi households;
- those reliant on state welfare benefits or living in rented accommodation.

Geographic concentration is another feature of financial exclusion in the UK; around 50 per cent of those financially excluded live in the 50 most deprived local authority districts.

Consequences of financial exclusion

Financial exclusion and the wider issues associated with access to finance are now of increasing global concern (see Peachey and Roe, 2004 and WSBI and World Bank, 2004). Although financial exclusion is not a new problem, its consequences are more serious than they were previously (FSA, 2000, p. 53). Having access to key financial products (a bank account, consumer credit, savings or insurance) can lead to many problems in a fast-changing, more demanding and competitive society.

Lack of banking facilities is especially problematic in an environment where a growing volume of payments are made via a bank account. Research has found that one of the top priority products for the financially excluded is an account to receive income and make payments (Kempson and Whyley, 1999).

Those without access to mainstream credit facilities may also face serious practical difficulties; credit needs cover both short-term facilities (to smooth peaks and troughs in household budgets) and different kinds of loans to buy larger items. As a result, the financially excluded are often incentivised to borrow from 'non-status lenders' who charge a high price. Since these loans are often secured on the borrower's property, the consequences of non-repayment are especially serious. In fact it may be worse and they may borrow from informal lenders such as loan-sharks who charge exorbitant rates and exact tough penalties if loans are not repaid.

Insurance exclusion becomes increasingly problematic as the range of risk cover possibilities extend. At the same time, the financially excluded are often most vulnerable to the kinds of risks that can be covered by insurance (ranging from home contents, mortgage protection to life cover and long-term sickness cover). The consequences of financial (and social) exclusion are, as a result, further heightened. The absence or inadequacy of pension provision carries with it the obvious consequence of a greater risk of poverty and hardship in later years. The impact of exclusion is heightened since membership of private pension schemes is increasingly becoming the norm. The Joseph Rowntree Foundation Inquiry (1995, p. 25) in the UK found that a 'substantial minority' of people were heavily reliant on the social security system. Those who are unable to manage on the income they receive in retirement face a very restricted range of available options.

A number of consequences flow from not having savings. The most fundamental of these is the loss of security and flexibility that the majority of people take for granted. As with insurance, the awareness of having no safety net is an ongoing source of concern for these financially excluded persons.

The preceding consequences of financial exclusion are not confined to individuals; they also impact on their communities. The withdrawal of financial services from certain localities (so-called 'financial desertification') has been associated with deterioration in the built environment, restricted economic growth and social problems (Leyshon and Thrift, 1994). Although first evident in the US, this decline process has more recently been observed in the UK:

> Holes are beginning to appear in the geography of retail financial services provision. ... The emergence of these spaces of financial exclusion has important implications for uneven development ... for such spaces are associated with economic decline and attendant social problems such as poverty and deprivation. (Leyshon and Thrift, 1995, pp. 313–314)

Leyshon and Thrift (1995, p. 315) go on to suggest that....'rich areas tend to get richer and poor areas poorer because of the way in which the financial system discriminates between people and communities on the basis of risk'.

Marshall *et al* (1999, p. 9) emphasise a related point that bears directly on the role and importance of local knowledge and presence by financial services firms:

> The loss of local information and knowledge may make financial institutions more cautious in their lending policy, because they will

come to rely on national lending models, thus restricting the flow of new investment into the area.

The marketing strategies of financial institutions based on the same geographical information systems may accelerate this 'desertification' (Thrift and Leyshon, 1997) of certain communities by mainstream financial providers.

US experiences

Experiences with financial exclusion in the US are similar to those in the UK. The most detailed and nationally representative survey of US household finances is the Survey of Consumer Finances (SCF), which is sponsored by the Board of Governors of the Federal Reserve System. This survey is conducted every three years.

In the 1998 SCF survey, about 9.5 per cent of all families in the US were without any kind of transactions (checking and/or savings) account. There was a significant decline in the percentage of families that had no transactions accounts between 1995 and 1998. The socio-economic groups most likely not to have transactions accounts were (disproportionately) likely to have low incomes, to be headed by someone younger than 35 or older than 75, to be headed by an unemployed, to be non-white or Hispanic and to be in the bottom 25 per cent of wealth distributions (FSA, 2000, p. 65). Except for cash-value life insurance and employer-provided pension accounts, families without transactions accounts are very unlikely to own any other financial asset.

US households generally use three kinds of credit: home-secured loans; installment loans; and revolving credit card loans. Like the UK, credit scoring is widely used to assess the creditworthiness of loan applicants. During the past two decades computerised databases and improved scoring methods have allowed lenders to classify credit applicants with greater precision. At the same time, more mainstream lenders have been willing to lend (at a higher price) to sub-prime applicants. This latter trend has markedly increased the ability of low-income households to access mainstream credit.

Despite these latter trends, however, low-income households are much less likely to have home-secured loans and they also have a reduced likelihood of holding installment loans (FSA, 2000, p. 66). The 1995 SCF found that 66.5 per cent of US households had at least one major credit card, but this dropped to 44.6 per cent for low-income families. Only 7.7 per cent of low-income families without transactions accounts had a major credit card. Similar patterns of financial exclusion are evident for other mainstream financial services in the US, like mortgages, pensions and savings-orientated life insurance.

US research finds a major reason that households do not have a transactions account is because they have practically no month-to-month financial savings. As a result, they do not feel that they need transactions accounts (FSA, 2000, p. 68). Other common reasons cited for not having transactions accounts are the extent of bank fees, minimum balance requirements, desire to keep financial records private and not feeling comfortable in dealing with a bank. The closing of bank branches in the 1980s has also been cited by many journalists and community activists as causing people to lose contact with banks and close their transactions accounts.

The consequences of exclusion are broadly similar to UK experiences summarised earlier. Caskey (1997) notes that in the majority of cases US 'unbanked' households can obtain alternative payment services with minimal difficulty or cost. Practically all households excluded from mainstream credit have alternative sources of credit, but these tend to be costly, inconvenient and provide poor consumer protection.

Responding to financial exclusion

This brief survey of US and UK experiences confirms that the causes of financial exclusions are several and complex. The barriers to inclusion are similarly varied and complicated, including apparently transparent barriers (like income) and more subtle ones (such as personal beliefs and prejudices). As a consequence, tackling financial exclusion is not easy. Both in the US and UK, however, there is a strong commitment from Government and the financial industry towards overcoming financial exclusion.

Although financial services firms have an important role to play, this may not be driven wholly by commercial, short-term profit motives. The FSA (2000, p. 79) survey emphasises the growing view that part-nerships – private/private; private/public; and private/not-for-profit – often offer the best route. It is unrealistic to expect that financial services firms alone are able to combat financial exclusion and this is one of the key messages from the present survey.

Increasing access to financial services has many aspects. These are summarised for the UK (FSA, 2000, Chapter 7) below:

- **Geographical access**

   Many believe that partnerships are especially important. These include banks working with supermarkets; The Post Office; and not-for-profit organisations (like credit unions, local exchange trading schemes (LETS) and various kinds of community bank). The present UK Government has strongly supported the development of the credit union movement. There has also been increasing interest in the development of community banks, mainly in response to branch closures by banks and building societies. The evidence to date (FSA, 2000, p. 82) suggests that LETS only have a marginal role to play in tackling financial exclusion. Many also believe that social landlords can play a key role in widening access to financial services in the UK.

- **Access for those with disabilities**

  Although most disabilities do not cause financial exclusion, they can increase the barriers faced by those who live on low incomes. One area of current concern in the UK (by The Office of Fair Trading) is how insurance companies justify differences in risk for those with disabilities. Whilst actuarial statistics may support different risk assessments, there is some evidence of over-zealous interpretation of insurance policy exclusions.

- **Risk assessment**

  We have outlined how developments in risk assessment can reduce access to many financial products. The Association of British Insurers argues that the current challenge is to find risk reduction practices and products that will widen access. One such example might be the design of a new type of bank account, a hybrid of the present UK chequing (current) and deposit (savings) accounts which does not carry an overdraft facility and, therefore, does not need to be credit scored (FSA, 2000, p. 84). A wide range of possibilities are being explored and developed, including new institutional and portfolio arrangements for handling risk assessment, management and sharing techniques.

- **Racism**

  Although there is little evidence to support racism in risk assessment, alleged racism increases financial exclusion. Several methods are used to tackle this problem, including attracting more staff from ethnic minority groups; better race awareness training of front-line staff; and ensuring compliance with the Race Relations Act, 1976.

- **Affordability**

  This is addressed through some of the methods discussed previously (like developing new, more suitable financial products). Simpler, 'plain vanilla' products should also be cheaper; they need also to be good value for money.

- **Financial literacy and psychological barriers**

  A significant barrier to the take-up of financial services is the existence of various psychological barriers. An apparent lack of suitable, available and understandable financial products has helped to fuel a mistrust and disinterest in financial services. This is being tackled via better information, more understandable details and some have argued for a free, independent advice service. The problems of deficient literacy and numeracy are also relevant.

- **Regulation and monitoring**

  Regulation and its interpretation have a role to play in financial exclusion. This covers areas like reducing proof of identity needs in opening a bank account to facilitating the growth of credit unions. New legislation is also demanded by some, drawing mainly on the example of the US Community Reinvestment Act, 1977. Many steps are also being taken to ensure the accurate monitoring of financial exclusion.

In the US, there have also been many public and private sector responses to the problem of financial exclusion. The Community Reinvestment Act, 1977, for example, includes a 'service test'. Banks are rated on their efforts and effectiveness at extending mortgage loans to low income households. These ratings come into play when banks ask for a regulatory ruling on requests like bank mergers. Other US initiatives include 'basic' or 'lifeline' bank account proposals; reducing the cost of switching; various moves to encourage savings in lower income groups; regulating loan policies of lenders in the alternative financial sector; and improved consumer education. One of the most influential books and policy proposals in this area is the work of Sherraden (1991), who proposed that government create Individual Development Accounts (IDAs). An IDA is designed to encourage low-income households to build up wealth by offering to match savings for approved purposes.

Conclusions

It is clear from recent US and UK experiences that financial exclusion is an important and growing challenge for policymakers and banks.

Furthermore, it is a complex concept with many often interrelated dimensions. The apparent growing importance of financial exclusion as a social and economic phenomenon in the US and UK also suggests that this kind of 'polarisation potential' is exacerbated by deregulation and the movement towards a more strongly market-orientated financial system. The following chapters explore in greater detail the modern experiences of the UK, US and other European experiences.

3
Financial Exclusion in the UK

Introduction

This chapter examines in greater detail modern UK experiences with financial exclusion. The UK has one of the most successful financial services industries in the world. A great deal of this is centred around the City of London, which *inter alia* houses more foreign banks than any other centre; has the largest foreign exchange market in the world; and is the largest market for over-the-counter derivatives. In this highly developed and innovative market environment, however, financial exclusion has become an increasing problem and a major policy issue for government and the private sector. Although there has generally been a steady increase in the use of most kinds of financial services in the UK during recent years, a minority of people have apparently become excluded (and in some cases more excluded) from financial services. The present chapter covers the following areas: the notion of excluded groups; barriers and consequences of financial exclusion; and initiatives that have been developed to tackle financial exclusion.

Financial exclusion in the UK and the nature of excluded groups

Background and types of indicators

In the UK, the FSA has undertaken a major survey of financial exclusion (FSA, 2000); this is the most comprehensive survey of the financial exclusion literature to date in the UK. At one level, this study is itself reflective of the FSA's growing role in seeking protection for consumers and promoting a greater public understanding of financial services and products. At a wider level, it also reflects the growing interest of Government, the financial services industry and society at large in financial exclusion. The new Labour Government provided an important impetus to this growing interest by the establishment of the Social Exclusion Unit (SEU). A number of Policy Action Teams (PATs) were set up by the SEU: one of these, PAT 14, was charged with examining financial exclusion and the FSA was heavily involved in this research (HM Treasury, 1999).

The UK Government's concern with financial exclusion is comparatively new. Up until recently, there has also been relatively little research on the causes and consequences of financial exclusion in the UK. In the past decade, however, a burgeoning literature has developed. During the term of the present Labour Government, financial exclusion has become recognised as one of the major issues facing disadvantaged communities.

Financial exclusion can be seen as part of the wider concept of social exclusion, which may be summarised as:

> a shorthand term for what can happen when people or areas suffer from a combination of linked problems such as unemployment, poor skills, low incomes, poor housing, high crime environment, bad health, poverty and family breakdown.   (FSA, 2000, p. 7)

These different aspects are often interrelated and mutually reinforcing. The *1999 Poverty and Social Exclusion Survey of Britain*, funded by the Joseph Rowntree Foundation, is the most detailed survey of social exclusion ever undertaken in the UK. It is also the first national study that attempted to measure social exclusion in an internationally comparable way: see Goodwin *et al* (2001). Social exclusion broadly covers those processes that result in a lack of economic, political or social citizenship. It is not the same as poverty, although the two appear to be closely related.

Financial exclusion was initially seen as a geographic phenomenon, but the FSA (2000) study found that it is a wider and more pervasive concept. There are also degrees, or levels, of financial exclusion. As we saw in Chapter 2, financial exclusion has many dimensions (access exclusion, condition exclusion, etc). Exclusion, then, can occur by risk assessment and the design of financial products; via the cost of a service in relation to income; through market segmentation; and by self-exclusion by those who either do not wish to access the financial system or believe that they will be denied financial services.

Recent years have seen the development of a mass market for financial services in the UK. However, at the time of the FSA (2000) survey, around seven per cent of households still lacked any financial product at all and a further 20 per cent were on the margin of financial services with barely more than a bank account. The likelihood of being on the margin also appears to be concentrated, both geographically and among certain groups in society. Financial exclusion has become an increasingly important part of the wider social exclusion debate in the UK (FSA, 2000, p. 9).

The Labour Government's Social Exclusion Unit only covers England. Similar moves, however, are under way in Scotland, Northern Ireland and Wales. The Scottish Social Inclusion Strategy, for example, has agreed a programme of action to be undertaken by five Social Inclusion Action Teams (Scottish Office, 1999). These teams cover between them local anti-poverty action; excluded young people; inclusive communities; evaluation and indicators; and 'making it happen' (using best practice models to help make recommendations about overcoming barriers to promoting social inclusion) (FSA, 2000, p. 8). The *New Targeting Social Need* initiative in Northern Ireland specifically targets social need and social exclusion (Northern Ireland Executive, 1999). In Wales, the NAW's (National Assembly for Wales) policy statement *Building an Inclusive Wales* sets out plans for monitoring annually changes in key indicators of exclusion in Wales (Welsh Office, 1999).

Financial exclusion is broadly defined as a state where people are not able to access mainstream financial services like banking facilities, credit cards and insurance policies, especially home insurance. There has been a steady increase in the use of all kinds of financial services in the UK during recent decades. Generally, more people now have access to a growing and more sophisticated array of financial services. At the same time, a minority of the population do not have even a basic bank or building society account. There are a number of indicators of financial exclusion, although not having a bank or building society account (either a cheque or a savings account) is a standard indicator of financial exclusion. It is estimated (BBA, 2002, p. 4) that not having access to basic banking services costs the most deprived members of the community an extra £5 a week each on average.

Practically, the extent of financial exclusion can be evaluated in terms of (Sinclair, 2001, Section 4):

- Levels of access to basic banking services for money transmission (e.g. current or chequing accounts);

- Levels of access to credit;
- Levels of access to insurance;
- Levels of debt and debt assistance;
- Levels of long term savings, the most important of which are pensions;
- Levels of financial literacy.

A particularly important factor is house ownership, which has a kind of double-edge significance for financial exclusion. On the one hand, it opens up wider access to mainstream financial services; on the other hand, it can itself be a source of problem debt.

One of the most prominent sources of financial exclusion indicators in the UK is the New Policy Institutes (NPI) annual studies on *Monitoring Poverty and Social Exclusion*. The NPI draws on three indicators of financial exclusion derived from extant Government data:

- the percentage of households without a bank or building society account;
- the percentage of households without household or home contents insurance;
- the percentage of households in mortgage arrears for over 12 months.

A summary of NPI's assessment of recent British trends in these three areas is shown in Table 3.1. However, there is no single definitive source to measure the extent of financial exclusion in Britain. As a result, estimates tend to vary across different studies and datasets (Sinclair, 2001, Section 4).

Figure 3.1 summarises some related indicators of financial exclusion from the 1999 Policy and Social Exclusion (PSE) survey in Britain: see Goodwin *et al* (2001). The PSE survey uses several questions that seek to quantify financial exclusion (Goodwin *et al*, 1999, p. 6):

- whether a household is currently or previously in debt during the past year;
- whether they have ever been disconnected from utilities (like water, gas, electricity) because of an inability to pay;
- whether they have had to borrow from sources other than a bank in the past year;
- whether the household is without access to a bank account;
- whether respondents are unable to save a small sum each month;
- whether the household has insurance on the contents of their dwellings.

The PSE (1999, p. 15) survey places these indicators into two groups: two indicators (not having a bank account or being able to afford home contents insurance) show direct exclusion from financial services and the rest concern debt and its various consequences. Figure 3.1 shows that the proportion of households who are financially excluded in these terms varies from 35 per cent of households with no savings to around five per cent who have been disconnected. The survey found that although the proportions excluded in each of these six indicators varied, the characteristics of those most likely to be excluded are generally the same (PSE, 1999, p. 14):

- households with no workers;
- lone-parent families;
- non-white households;
- households receiving IS (income support) or JSA (Job Seekers Allowance);
- households with younger respondents;
- households living in local authority housing;
- households with respondents who left education at an early age;
- households in more densely populated areas.

Other surveys support these household characteristics as being most commonly associated with financial exclusion.

Another survey of financial exclusion in Britain was conducted in three areas of London during early 2002. This survey was especially interesting because it examined financial exclusion from the view point of both access to banking services and the use of alternative (more expensive) financial services; Table 3.2 summarises the results. The study demonstrated that the risk of financial exclusion is closely correlated with household circumstances. This obtained in a population that is distinguished by low household incomes and in urban areas that are still serviced by mainstream banks. This same study suggested that the following factors are associated with financial exclusion:

- low household incomes;
- using expensive sources of credit;
- borrowing to pay for day-to-day living expenses;
- having no savings;
- no access to cheapest fuel tariffs;
- concern about getting into debt;

Table 3.1　New Policy Institute analysis of recent trends in financial exclusion 1997–1999

	Over a 5-year period	*Over latest year of available data*	*Approximate numbers affected in latest years*	*Variations across groups*
% without a bank of building society account	Steady	Steady	N/A	The poorest fifth of the population is more than three times as likely not to have an account as those on average incomes
% without home contents insurance	N/A	Steady	N/A	Households without insurance are nearly twice as likely to be burgled as those with insurance
% in mortgage arrears for 12 months	Improved	Improved	45,000	N/A

Source: CRISIS (2001, Section 4)

- dependence of means-tested state benefits;
- caring responsibilities that constrain the ability to work; and
- work in insecure and low income occupations.

Other research by Bridges and Disney (1992) also support these same findings.

Another study carried out by the Office of Fair Trading (OFT) (1999) and summarised in their report *Left Out in the Cold* researched the cir-

Figure 3.1   Indicators of financial exclusion

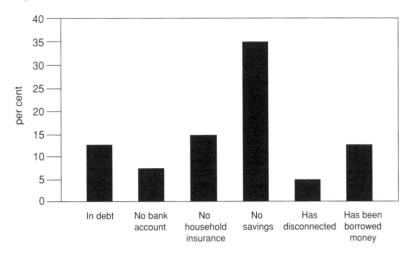

Source: CRSP (1999, Figure 21, p. 7)

cumstances of six million households, defined as 'having low or very low household incomes': see also Drakeford and Sachdev (2001). The research found that of these six million:

- two million had no current account in the household;
- 3.5 million did not use any form of credit;
- two million lacked home contents insurance;
- three million did not have either long- or short-term savings products;
- 4–5 million were without life insurance products in the previous five years;
- 2.5 million had received no sales contacts from financial services firms during the past 14 months.

Drakeford and Sachdev (2001, p. 215) emphasise a key finding of the report that 'current banking and insurance practices are excluding millions of households from essential financial services'.

The Lothian Anti Poverty Alliance (LAPA, April 2002) report similar indicators of financial exclusion in the UK:

- 7.9 million in the UK are financially excluded. These are systematically refused credit by mainstream lenders and they represent a £16 billion market;

Table 3.2   Access to financial services by selected household types

Access to financial services	Total %	Lone parent %	Household with children %	Household with disabled etc %	Workless households %
Current account	76	60	73	71	63
Debt or guarantee card	58	38	55	53	39
Credit card	38	18	36	35	24
Store card	24	14	25	19	16
Loan from finance company or moneylender	11	21	15	10	14
Catalogue purchase loans	20	33	24	25	22
Some form of borrowing	54	63	60	57	47

Source: Community Finance Solutions, University of Salford, March 2002

- Around 1.5 million households, have no mainstream financial services;
- A further 1 in 5 make very little use of financial services (1 in 10 have just one financial product and a further 1 in 10 have only two products);
- Levels of non-use are highest in Scotland: 13 per cent of households are without any financial products.

The annual report of the BBA (2002) reports several headline statistics of financial exclusion, including:

- Between 20–25 per cent of household in the UK (around 6 million people) do not have home contents insurance.
- Around 95 per cent of adults have access to a bank or building society account; of these, about 82 per cent have a current account.
- Approximately one in four adults in Britain does not have a private or occupational pension.

- Well over 30 per cent of households do not have savings or investment products.

Once financially excluded, households and individuals apparently become 'trapped'; they are unable to exit and become increasingly subject to cycles of debt.

Why is financial exclusion occurring in the UK?

Deregulation and increased competition in the UK financial services sector have produced many apparent economic benefits (Gardener *et al*, 2002). For example, a greater variety of new and novel financial products and services have been produced. With the concomitant rise of a more market-orientated financial services sector, financial services firms (FSFs) are incentivised to respond more strongly to the 'needs satisfying demands' of customers. Within this deregulation process, there has been greater potential for financial inclusion: people have access to a wider variety of products and services. At the same time, there have been important social and economic changes that appear to have resulted in greater exclusion.

However, with this process of deregulation, intensifying competition and generally more financial inclusion, the problems of financial exclusion have paradoxically worsened. While average incomes have risen markedly in the UK since 1979, the real incomes of the poorest 10 per cent have fallen significantly (for example, they fell by eight per cent between 1979 and 1994/95). Brewer *et al* (2003, p. 21) in a recent Institute for Fiscal Studies study also report on increasing UK income inequality alongside increasing redistribution. The growth of poverty has been a fundamental cause of financial exclusion.

Under the general heading of social and income changes, we can list several factors (FSA, 2000, ch. 2). Incomes and income distribution are clearly important. Whilst the incomes of the richest 10 per cent of the population grew by 60–68 per cent between 1979 and 1994/95, those of the poorest decile grew by only 10 per cent without taking housing costs into account; when these latter costs are included, the poorest decile's income fell by eight per cent over this same period. After allowing for labour mobility, the Joseph Rowntree Foundation (1995, 1998) conclude that between 80 and 90 per cent of those in the poorest income group are characterised by long-term poverty.

As noted already, in the UK the types of people who are likely to experience financial exclusion of some kind appear to be (see Sinclair [2001, ch. 6] and FSA [2000, p. 12]):

- the long-term unemployed;
- old age pensioners (especially those aged over 70);
- those unable to work because of sickness or long-term disability;
- people in low wage employment;
- young householders who have not yet used financial services;
- female single parents;
- a disproportionate number of people from minority ethnic groups (especially African-Caribbean, Pakistani, and Bangladeshi people).

The Joseph Rowntree Foundation (1995, 1998) also found that the majority of those financially excluded live in social rented housing. Those reliant on state welfare benefits or who are living in rented accommodation (more likely conditions in the above listed sub-groups) are also more likely to experience some form of financial exclusion.

The distinguishing, thematic characteristic of the above group is low income: this is the single factor that is most closely associated with financial exclusion. Excluding self-exclusion, the order of factors that best predict financial exclusion broadly defined are listed below (Sinclair, 2001, ch. 6):

- those claiming means-tested benefits;
- people on low incomes;
- households where the head has been unemployed for a period;
- tenants occupying rented accommodation;
- single non-pensioners;
- those from Pakistani or Bangladeshi communities;
- those leaving school before age sixteen.

Although the types of people on low incomes in the UK have not changed much in the three decades up to the 1990's, there have been some important proportional shifts. Pensioners, for example, have dropped to around 20 per cent of low income households compared to over 50 per cent in the late 1960s. Although this is likely to change, for instance, a Pensions Commission (2004) report found that more than 12 million working people in the UK are not saving enough for their retirement and if taxes, savings or retirement ages were not increased, pensioners would suffer a 30 per cent decline in relative incomes.

Although income inequality is an important factor in its own right for explaining financial exclusion, the reasons for income inequality and changes in the composition of the population are equally important. These include changes in the labour market, demography, housing policy, social security and fiscal policy. We will merely summarise these often complex and interrelated change: see FSA (2000, ch. 2) and Sinclair (2001, ch. 6).

Labour market changes may be summarised (FSA, 2000, pp. 12 & 13) below:

- the gap between low and high pay has grown rapidly during the past two decades;
- these has been a growth in the 'flexible' labour market (i.e. jobs that are not full-time and permanent);
- a rapid decline has occurred in the number of employees who have their wages paid in cash;
- there has been a large increase during the past few decades in the number and proportion of women in the labour market.

Demographic factors have also been important. The most important of these are the growth in the number of single parents, people living independently at a younger age and the fact that more people than ever before are living longer.

Housing policy and shifts in tenure are significant factors in explaining financial exclusion. For one thing, there has been a marked increase in the number of households owning their own home. A consequence has been the 'residualisation' of social housing: a greater concentration of lower income households in the social housing sector (Sinclair, 2001, Section 6.3). Around 80 per cent of financially excluded householders live in council or housing association accommodation (Sinclair, 2001, Section 6.3). There is also a geographic dimension to financial exclusion; around 50 per cent of those financially excluded live in the 50 most deprived boroughs in the UK (Joseph Rowntree Foundation, 1999).

Growing home ownership has had several important effects on financial services. For one thing, it increases the demand for services like mortgages and insurance. Householders are also able to borrow more easily against the equity in their property. These effects, though, increase the range, variety and access to services of those with some wealth; they do nothing to mitigate the problems of the financially excluded. At the same time, increasing debt burdens associated with mortgages and increased borrowing may increase financial pressures on mortgagees; the number of properties repossessed by lenders in the UK has grown markedly during recent years. Growing risk of debt can itself become a process leading to financial exclusion.

Welfare and fiscal reform have undoubtedly contributed to the income inequalities noted earlier. These reforms have themselves been associated with an increased 'privatisation' of services previously provided by the state. In this climate, FSFs (financial services firms) have been encouraged to develop a wider variety of new savings, pensions and insurance-type products to help fill the gaps left by these reforms. (In fact the lack of success of the take-up of private pension schemes is one reason for the impending UK pension crisis as noted above). Access to these services in the open market, however, is far from uniform and is dictated by price – access is not decided ultimately by real social need.

We saw at the start of this section that important developments in UK financial services markets have increased the array of financial services available. Deregulation and intensifying competition have helped to break down traditional institutional and specialist boundaries between historically segmented financial institutions, thereby facilitating the development of more generic FSFs. There was also a big influx of new entrants into the financial services industry. At the same time, developments in information technology (IT) began to change the economics of financial services markets.

One result of this process was that the new and more intense competition required a continuous search for new customers. Creation of new, generic products, mass marketing and 'factory style' processing of product sales and data became common. Using customer data as information in product development and delivery evolved as a major strategic need and a competitive weapon. FSFs use these data to help segment their business: geographically, by products and by customer characteristic.

The deregulation requirement of shareholder value maximisation has increasingly driven FSF business. As a result, the need to understand and price more closely on a market-determined risk and return basis became paramount. Explicit pricing and the elimination of previously hidden (in price) cost subsidisation became the norm. Credit risk appraisal and monitoring systems became more important and their sophistication increased with IT and related developments. Recent years have witnessed a movement towards greater market-orientated, risk-based pricing and bank performance appraisal using techniques like RAROC (Risk Adjusted Return on Capital) and BVA (Break-up Value Analysis). The new, developing Basel 2 system for capital adequacy (with its emphasis on economic capital and more sophisticated, market-based risk management techniques) will further intensify these kinds of trends.

Many of the new competitors were able to 'cherry pick' attractive, less risky customer segments since they understood their customers via other schemes and products (e.g. like loyalty cards). Unlike the established banks and other traditional financial institutions, many of these new competitors were able to operate without having their own branch networks; they were also able to market more effectively on the basis of a recognised brand. All of these developments helped to develop a process of segmentation and tiering of customers by risk and other characteristics. This segmentation and tiering process was especially marked during the 1990s. These segmentation moves are apparently intensifying. Recent press attention (*Daily Mail*, October 20, 2003) alleges that banks and other financial services firms' call centres are prioritising wealthier customers in their speed and level of response.

The pressures to cut costs became marked in the new deregulation era. Cost structures built up during the pre-deregulation area (when traditional financial institutions were effectively 'protected' from competition by regulation) became unsustainable. At the same time, the decision-making process became more centralised in banking and financial services.

Banks sought to reduce costs by closing branches; local knowledge and credit information were correspondingly weakened. At the same time, the pressures of competition drove banks to target more heavily their most profitable customers. Both of these developments tended to disenfranchise (exclude) their poorer customers, especially those located in poorer and less populated locations. This uneven spatial pattern of branch closures and focussing on deprived urban areas has been referred to a 'financial desertification' (FSA, 2000, para 2.59).

This process increased the need for clear, transparent and homogenous indicators of customer probity and potential profitability (to the FSF). The trend was further fuelled by the introduction in 1993 of stricter rules to combat money laundering; these required various proof of identity (including social and economic status) before a person is able to open a bank account. Inevitably, they also operated to discriminate further against many groups of persons, leading to more financial exclusion.

Superimposed on all of these developments was the 1990s debt crisis in the UK, which was preceded by the lesser developed countries (LDC) debt crisis of the 1980s. From this time, periodic financial crisis and the growing pressures of capital adequacy regulation encouraged a 'flight to quality' in financial services (Leyshon and Thrift, 1995). Although many of the preceding trends (like the growth of a bigger mass market in financial services) increased financial inclusion, the need and means to price risk more accurately meant that those who were outside acceptable risk tolerance levels became more financially excluded. At the same time, increasing market segmentation exacerbated this trend. For insurance products, increased market segmentation led to smaller risk pools and higher risk premia.

This process of polarisation in access to financial services has been accompanied by a process of 'information exclusion' (FSA, 2000, para 2.49). The same information and data used to classify individuals into risk bands are also used to market financial products and services. As a result, there is a marked divide in information provision by FSFs for different kinds of customers. The more profitable customers effectively become 'super included'; an even more marked polarisation develops between these and the increasingly excluded segments.

The overall impact of these changes in UK financial services markets has been the development of *inter alia* a mass market, clearer product branding, risk-based pricing, more customer segmentation and pressures to cut costs. Generally, this has led to greater financial inclusion. People are using a wider array of financial services. At the same time, some segments of society have become more financially excluded; the gap between those financially excluded and included has apparently widened. In short, the financially excluded have become more polarised. The FSA survey (2000, para 2.62) observes that ... 'financial service providers, by and large, have not responded to the needs of people where profit levels will be lower'. Nor have they responded to important shifts like the growing 'flexibility' of the labour market.

Excluded groups and products

We have discussed in some detail the kinds of people who apparently suffer from financial exclusion. All of the studies to date suggest that financial exclusion is concentrated both geographically and in certain groups of people (FSA, 2000, para 3.3). At the same time, no single factor accounts for financial exclusion (Sinclair, 2001, Section 7.1). Outright refusal of FSFs to provide any financial service is still rare. On the other hand, as we have seen, FSFs (until recently) have not made significant efforts to help deprived and disadvantaged groups. In this section we explore in a little more detail the main reasons for financial exclusion and the respective financial products involved.

It is already clear from the preceding analysis that financial exclusion arises as a result of many factors and these can be interrelated and complex. It is also clear that financial exclusion should be taken to include those groups who are at the margin of financial services (i.e. they are not totally excluded). The concept may also be extended to include those groups who are financially 'included', but are discriminated against in terms of the level of service received and ease of access to more 'attractive' financial products. For the moment, though, we will focus more on those excluded in the stricter sense: that is, groups who have no financial services or who are at the margin of financial services. The preceding analysis shows that financial exclusion in these terms appears to be concentrated, both geographically and amongst particular groups.

Table 3.3 summarises numbers of financial products by household circumstances and Table 3.4 shows numbers of financial products by socio-economic circumstances. Individuals and households on low incomes are most likely to be at the lowest end of engagement in financial services. This includes especially lone parents, the unemployed, those who cannot work because of long-term sickness, or disability and the elderly on incomes of less than £150 per week: see FSA (2000, p. 22). Income is a much more important factor in exploring financial exclusion than age *per se*.

Kempson and Whyley (1999b) show statistically that low income significantly increases the likelihood of being financially excluded. Being a woman also appears to intensify the impact of being on a low income and attempting to access financial services (FSA, 2000, para 3.11). But low income alone is not a complete explanation, despite its singular importance. FSA (2000, para 3.12), for example, confirm the importance of low income in explaining financial exclusion for African-Caribbean's, but for Pakistanis and Bangladeshis in the UK language, culture and religion are also important factors.

There are many apparent reasons why individuals do not hold a bank or building society chequing-type account. Those who have never had an account include (FSA, 2000, para 3.30):

• those who never needed one and use a savings account instead;
• young people who have yet to open an account;
• women who have always relied on their husband's account;
• women who became single mothers at a young age; and
• those who prefer a cash budget (many of these believe that they would be rejected if they applied for an account).

Those who have had an account in the past typically close it after a fall in income (e.g. following a job loss, retirement or long-term sickness).

Financial exclusion is also geographically concentrated. In the UK, financial exclusion is highest in Scotland (13 per cent of households have no financial products and a further 25 per cent only one or two). The North, North West, Greater London and Wales are also characterised by higher than average levels of financial exclusion (FSA, 2000, para 3.4). Kempson and Whyley (1999a) show that these differences cannot be explained statistically by differing economic circumstances. Living in more deprived local authorities is positively correlated with higher financial exclusion. The Bristol University Personal Finance Research Centre found that the majority (around 80 per cent) of those financially excluded live in council or housing association accommodation; half of these live in the 50 most deprived UK boroughs. Several studies have identified a 'desertification' of financial services from areas of very low income. This appears to create and/or intensify physical and psychological boundaries to using financial services in the populations affected (FSA, 2000, para 3.16).

Geographical access to banking services appears to be important in explaining financial exclusion. There have been recurring concerns in the UK during recent years about the growing number of bank branch closures. These branch closures have typically been concentrated in low income and deprived areas. Nevertheless, there are around 12,000 retail bank branches in the UK and 85 per cent of the urban population still live within a mile of the nearest bank branch, and 85 per cent of the rural population within four miles. The BBA (2003, p. 5) report that the rate of branch closures has slowed in the UK. During 2001, for example, the number of bank branches reduced by less that one per cent. Despite this, around two per cent of the population faced real difficulties in getting to a branch and have apparently reduced their use of financial services (FSA, 2000, para 3.40). In general, restricted access to branches and other outlets for financial services may exacerbate formidable psychological boundaries to banking.

Banking and/or building society chequing accounts have been the subject of a considerable amount of research in the context of financial exclusion. These accounts are typically the 'apex' of the pyramid of financial services access and use by individuals. With savings products, self-exclusion appears to be the main reason for not holding such an account; many people with low incomes simply cannot afford to save. The group (especially low income and ethnic minority groups) who are less likely to save in financial accounts are more likely to save through

Table 3.3   Numbers of financial products by socio-economic circumstances

						row percentages	
			Number of financial products[a]				
	None	Low	Medium-Low	Average	Medium-High	High	Weighted Base
	%	%	%	%	%	%	
All households	7	19	20	11	21	22	26,435
Age of household head (years)							
16–19	26	57	13	2	2	–	112
20–29	11	27	18	11	19	15	3,211
30–39	6	16	15	11	26	26	5,272
40–49	4	11	15	11	25	34	4,738
50–59	5	13	17	11	23	32	3,982
60–69	6	18	24	13	19	19	3,813
70–79	7	27	29	13	15	9	3,522
80+	10	39	27	8	10	6	1,785
Household type							
Single, no children	11	25	20	11	19	14	3,581
Couple, no children	2	10	15	12	28	33	4,515
Three+ adults, no children	1	10	18	12	26	32	1,911
Single pensioner	12	37	28	9	9	5	4,132
Couple pensioners	3	16	27	15	21	18	3,783
Lone parent	23	42	17	7	7	4	1,790
Couple with children	3	11	14	10	27	35	5,861
Three+ adults with children	3	11	20	12	24	30	862
Ethnicity							
White	6	19	20	11	21	23	25,215
Black	16	37	22	8	11	7	440
Indian	3	17	26	16	18	19	282
Pakistani/Bangladeshi	14	42	29	7	6	2	211
Other	7	29	21	8	21	14	287
Age completed education (HoH, years)							
16 or under	8	23	22	11	19	16	19,151
17–19	3	11	15	11	26	35	4,084
20+	–	7	12	10	25	45	2,939
Housing tenure							
Owned outright	–	11	29	15	24	20	6,818
Mortgagor	–	1	12	14	33	40	10,605
Local authority tenant	23	51	19	4	2	–	5,348
Housing association	20	50	23	4	2	1	1,190
Private tenant	9	39	28	10	10	5	2,474

.aim on a particular policy are correspondingly most likely to
:d.

xclusion from insurance is rare; affordability is the most
: factor in explaining lack of insurance. More risk-sensitive
insurance products has meant that cover is more expensive
risky groups. Another factor is that insurance may be un-
: to some groups because of the kind of insurance policy
An example would be a home contents policy with a
. level of cover that exceeds the cover required. Another
: factor is that people with low incomes usually cannot pay
nce in a way that matches their budget. For example,
annual premium may be too onerous and using a monthly
it is not feasible without a basic account as well. Other
plaining lack of insurance include the conditions attached
: and/or a lack of knowledge about what is available on the

Treasury estimates that around 27 per cent of all employees
: members of occupational pension schemes nor have personal
(FSA, 2000, para 3.96). The reasons for not having a private
making inadequate pension provision include lack of oppor-
k of interest, lack of disposable income, lack of knowledge and
of pension providers, and religious and cultural factors are
for some ethnic minorities (FSA, 2000, para 3.105).

o credit is often perceived to be central to the financial exclu-
te. One reason for this concern is that borrowing (whilst
:ssary) invariably exacerbates the problems that low-income
:e. Indeed, the impact of credit is pervasive in the sense that
and 'misuse' impacts on all groups that access financial ser-
he wider context of financial exclusion, some groups with
financial services are excluded (via credit scoring, bank cus-
mentation strategies etc.) from various kinds and levels of
vertheless, the use of credit has grown strongly and is now
. Only a relatively small proportion (though apparently
is without access to any form of credit. Nevertheless, those
from mainstream financial services are often forced to seek
:nsive sources, (like money lenders, pawnbrokers, mail order
and cheque cashers).

.as been a marked growth in both the volume and different
:redit available in the UK market during recent years. High
nancial innovation, intense competition, aggressive market-
:er sophistication in credit risk appraisal, the pursuit of cus-

Table 3.3   Numbers of financial products by socio-economic
circumstances (cont'd)

						row percentages
	None	Low	Medium-Low	Average	Medium-High	High	Weighted Base
	%	%	%	%	%	%	
Standard region							
North, including Cumbria	9	25	22	13	19	13	1,619
Yorkshire and Humberside	6	21	22	11	20	20	2,305
North West	9	21	20	12	20	19	2,921
East Midlands	5	19	19	12	22	23	1,926
West Midlands	6	20	20	11	21	22	2,407
East Anglia	4	17	19	12	25	23	1,067
Greater London	9	23	20	10	19	19	2,961
South East (excluding London)	3	14	17	11	24	32	5,119
South West	4	17	20	11	23	27	2,297
Scotland	13	25	19	10	19	15	2,358
Wales	8	23	25	12	18	14	1,455
Local levels of deprivation[b]							
1 (most deprived)	11	27	20	11	16	15	5,699
2	7	23	23	11	21	16	3,931
3	5	19	21	13	24	20	2,406
4	4	15	20	13	23	25	2,440
5	4	13	18	11	23	31	2,416
6	2	13	16	11	24	34	2,157
7 (least deprived)	2	13	17	11	24	34	3,573

The columns are headed *Number of financial products[a]*.

a   Low: 1 or 2 products; Medium-Low: 3 or 4 products; Average: 5 products; Medium-high: 6 or 7 products; High: 8 or more products.
b   Analysis based on the Department of the Environment, Transport and Regions (DETR) *Deprivation Index* and restricted to England and Wales.
HoH: Head of Household
Base: all households 22,622
Source: FSA (2000, Table 3.1)

informal methods. ROSCA's (Rotating Savings and Credit Schemes)
and credit unions appear to be more prominent amongst minority
ethnic communities (FSA, 2000, paras 3.69 and 3.70).

Insurance access has been prominent in financial exclusion
research: see, for example, (Kempson & Whyley [1999b], FSA [2000],
and Sinclair [2001]). The numbers of UK households without particular

Table 3.4   Numbers of financial products by household circumstances

row percentages

| | Number of financial products[a] | | | | | | |
	None	Low	Medium-Low	Average-High	Medium	High	Weighted Base
	%	%	%	%	%	%	
All households	7	19	20	11	21	22	26,435
Net weekly household income							
No income	2	18	17	13	22	27	*179*
£1–50	6	26	28	13	18	9	*321*
£51–100	16	39	29	6	8	3	*2,785*
£101–I50	16	37	26	10	9	4	*4,490*
£151–200	9	29	25	13	17	8	*3,665*
£201–300	4	15	22	16	26	18	*5,279*
£301–400	–	6	16	12	34	32	*3,631*
£400–500	–	3	8	10	31	48	*2,276*
more than £500	–	1	6	7	26	60	*3,193*
Net equivalent weekly household income							
No income	2	18	17	13	22	27	*179*
£1–50	4	19	24	16	23	14	*213*
£51–100	8	28	32	9	16	7	*191*
£101–I50	15	35	29	9	9	4	*4,058*
£151–200	13	34	23	10	13	6	*5,282*
£201–300	4	17	22	14	25	19	*6,769*
£301–400	1	7	14	12	32	35	*3,976*
£400–500	–	3	10	11	30	47	*2,127*
more than £500	–	2	6	8	25	59	*2,433*
Receipt of income-related benefit							
None	–	8	20	14	28	31	*18,289*
Council Tax Benefit only	2	24	39	13	15	6	*1,229*
Income Support only	4	18	27	13	21	18	*589*
Council Tax Benefit & Income Support	3	32	40	13	9	3	*974*
Housing Benefit only	13	62	21	2	2	–	*484*
Housing Benefit & Council Tax Benefit	21	58	17	3	1	–	*1,403*
Housing Benefit & Income Support	36	49	9	2	3	2	*365*
Housing Benefit, Council Tax Benefit & Income Support	35	55	9	–	–	–	*3.102*

Table 3.4   Numbers of financial products (cont'd)

	Number of		
	None	Low	Medium-Low
	%	%	%
Economic activity status (HoH)			
Self employed	–	6	16
Full-time employment	–	9	16
Part-time employment	6	29	22
Unemployed	19	38	20
Retired	8	29	28
Sick/disabled	19	32	22
Student	8	40	28
Other inactive	22	32	14
No. of years since last worked (HoH)			
0	–	9	16
1	8	31	22
2	10	29	23
3	13	25	22
4	13	29	22
5	10	31	23
6–10	13	27	25
11–16	12	32	27
21 or more	16	39	25

a   Low: 1 or 2 products; Medium-Low: 3 or 4 prod
    6 or 7 products; High: 8 or more products.
    HoH: Head of Household.
Base: all *households 22,622.*
Source: FSA (2000, Table 3.2)

types of insurance (from a 1998 surve
para 3.73):

- 26 per cent had no home contents in
- 87 per cent no mortgage payment pr
- 91 per cent no medical insurance;
- and 93 per cent no personal acciden

The characteristics of those without i
kind of insurance involved. Generally

likely to
be exclue

Direct
importa
pricing c
for more
affordab
available
minimu
importa
for insu
paying a
direct de
factors e
to polici
market.

The U
are neith
pensions
pension
tunity, la
mistrust
importa

Access
sion deb
often ne
groups fa
credit us
vices. In
access to
tomer se
credit. N
the nor
growing
exclude
more ex
catalogu

There
kinds of
rates of
ing, grea

tomer segmentation strategies, greater sophistication in risk-based pricing and more emphasis on shareholder value maximisation in FSF strategies are some of the key features of the UK mass market in credit. As we saw earlier, these developments have apparently exacerbated the polarisation of access to financial services.

Compared with other kinds of financial services, there are much higher rates of 'denied access' to mainstream credit (FSA, 2000, para 3.137). People are unable to access mainstream financial services for many reasons. Non-status borrowers (who have a poor or non-existent credit history), for example, are unable to obtain mainstream credit facilities. These borrowers are also often 'encouraged' to pursue non-status borrowing via less strict lending criteria of non-mainstream lenders, extensive media advertising and lack of knowledge of alternatives. Mainstream lenders may also be unable to meet their needs. These borrowers are typically seeking small sums of money for relatively short periods of time.

Barriers to financial inclusion

It is clear that different 'groups' of people may be unable to access particular kinds of financial products for many reasons. There is no single factor that explains financial exclusion and no unique solution is feasible for all kinds of exclusion. It is also the case that even in relatively deprived and isolated communities, outright refusal to provide services by financial institutions is rare.

Nevertheless, until quite recently, financial institutions have not expended great efforts to help service economically vulnerable and marginalised groups (Sinclair, 2001, Section 7). A basic problem is often the mismatch between the products on offer and potential customers' needs (HM Treasury, 1999, p. 1).

FSA (2000, p. 46) identifies various kinds of barriers to inclusion within the financial services sector. These include the following:

- access difficulties
- lack of appropriate financial products
- affordability
- lack of appropriate delivery mechanisms
- poor levels of knowledge
- psychological barriers, including a mistrust of suppliers
- language and cultural problems
- the impact of legislation and regulation

These barriers do not apply to all financial products and, where they do, they can differ considerably in their nature and impact. There are many different kinds of access barrier, including geographical access, access for those with disabilities, risk assessment, racism and marketing. Geographic (or physical) access has been restricted in poorer communities where the level of basic branch provision is comparatively low. It is also the case that those societal groups that are especially prone to financial exclusion are also those that find it more difficult to get to a more remote bank branch. These groups are also more resistant to cash machines or ATMs and have less access to them: see, for example Kempson and Jones (2000) and Thrift and Leyshon (1997). These same groups often feel more comfortable using a building society or Post Office. Many small local building societies are also reluctant to close branches and are more committed to their local community (FSA, 2000, p. 46). This 'regional identity' (with an associated greater knowledge and strategic concern with regional development) is a feature of traditional UK building societies.

Geographic access has also been affected by cost cutting pressures in the insurance sector. One such area is the method of selling insurance directly to householders via a salesman calling at each home; the same technique was also used to collect premiums. Lower income families and other societal groups (like those with physical disabilities) were better able to access basic insurance services through these means. However, many companies no longer use this mode of service delivery.

Many physical disabilities comprise barriers to inclusion. These vary from mobility through to sight, hearing and other impediments. As a result, people with these kinds of disabilities may be unable to read ATM screens or use telephone-based services.

Risk assessment, as we discussed earlier, is another area that can provide a barrier to financial services. On the one hand, more accurate risk analysis and related pricing have increased inclusion; financial products can be tailored and priced on a more accurate economic basis so as to make them available to a wider clientele. On the downside, though, more accurate and detailed risk screening operates by definition against those groups who are more 'risky' in a credit scoring context: like low income groups, people living in deprived neighbourhoods and those with a history of poor payment. The impact of modern risk assessment methods varies between different kinds of financial product. For example, the impact of risk assessment is more evident in consumer credit, whilst 'affordability' is more relevant to insurance access (FSA, 2000, pp. 47–48).

More focussed marketing and greater sophistication in segmenting customers can also exacerbate exclusion. Modern marketing techniques and associated customer (actual and potential) information data files allow FSFs to target much more selectively. The result is that those at the margins of inclusion are unlikely to be targeted for promotional literature of new and existing financial products. As a result, a growing asymmetric information gap develops between those excluded and financial product providers (Leyshon *et al*, 1998).

Racism is another apparent barrier. There is evidence that some financial service staff may discriminate against ethnic minority groups (FSA, 2000, para 4.17). Nevertheless, no clear evidence supports the allegation that banks and other credit firms are racist in their credit granting.

Within the financial services industry, there have been periodic 'flights to quality'. These have increased the banking importance of more accurate credit screening and avoiding clusters of customers who are 'financially fragile'. One result has been the development of a wider range of more tailored and sophisticated products for profitable customer groups. As a result, the gap between the financially included (supplied with a greater variety of new products than ever before) and those excluded (increasingly discriminated against on the basis of their credit risk potential) widens. The same product innovation effort expended on wealthier customer groups is not devoted towards the design, testing and delivery of more appropriate products for lower income and other excluded groups.

Many products developed for lower income groups have since been withdrawn. These include, for example, indemnity home contents insurance that allows cover for second-hand replacements of damaged or stolen possessions and budgeting accounts that allow individuals to spread costs. Another such 'product gap' is borrowing for short periods with a weekly (and sometimes varying) pattern of repayments. Relatively large deposits may also be needed to open new savings accounts. Although many low income groups save regularly via life insurance, there is widespread agreement that this is not a suitable kind of savings product for those with a low and/or fluctuating income stream (FSA, 2000, para 4.23). Lack of transparency and inflexibility are also factors that are important in not taking out a private pension. Several studies have also drawn attention to a lack of financial products that accord with Islamic requirements (HM Treasury, 1999).

Affordability is a serious barrier. Those with low incomes face a corresponding reduced ability to access any but the most basic and cheapest of financial products. At the same time, low income groups often have to pay more because of their lower credit standing. This 'double-edged sword' can be a major barrier. Another aspect is the reduced ability of those without a bank account to spread the costs of home contents insurance (FSA, 2000, para 4.29).

Methods of service delivery can also be important (Joseph Rowntree Foundation, 1999). Sinclair (2001, Section 7.9) suggests that telephone banking is obviously of little use to those without a telephone! The BBA (2003, p. 6) points out that of the 12,000 or so retail bank branches in the UK, over 1,000 provide customers with access to the Internet. Nevertheless, the rise of Internet banking will also discriminate against those households without a PC or access to one. Generation attitudes (the older generation prefer more overt means of banking) and technology-literacy may also be relevant barriers in this context.

Financial literacy has several aspects. Research shows that consumers often do not have the information and/or expertise to make informed decisions about purchasing financial products. Even more sophisticated included groups are often 'challenged' in choosing amongst the many financial options offered to them. This problem is exacerbated for those on the margin of mainstream financial services; not only may they lack basic financial literacy, but they also may be unaware of even viable (for them) products available. Research has shown that financial literacy and exclusion often begin in early childhood: see FSA (2000, para 4.31) and FSA (2000a).

Psychological barriers and mistrust of suppliers can also be effective barriers. Lack of knowledge is often associated with generalised mistrust of financial services firms by those on the periphery of mainstream financial services. Banks are often seen as being uninterested in those with low incomes, although building societies are often viewed as more helpful. Many people on low incomes save through informal means. Insurance companies probably have the most negative image (FSA, 2000, para 4.36). The publicity surrounding the mis-selling of pensions and endowment policies increased the distrust of financial services providers. The perceived inadequate response by UK regulators to these scandals has not helped to mitigate this distrust.

Language and cultural barriers also appear to be significant, especially for those from Pakistani and Bangladeshi communities (FSA, 2000, para 4.38). These barriers appear strongest for first generation immigrants.

Finally, the impact of Government policy and regulation can lead to barriers. We saw earlier, for example, that money laundering regulations have had the unintended effect of restricting access to banking. The regulation of savings and investment product selling and social security regulations on means testing have restricted access to financial products. The system of social security benefits payable in cash has helped to encourage recipients to remain unbanked. Without a basic banking facility, other financial products are invariably less easily accessed.

Consequences of financial exclusion

There are many consequences of financial exclusion. Although, on balance a higher proportion of the UK population is now financially included compared with earlier times, we have seen that apparent polarisation of the financially excluded has increased. At the same time, the consequences of not being able to access basic financial products (bank account, consumer credit, insurance and long-term investments or a pension) are more serious when the majority of households have these products. With this kind of polarisation, the more general problems of social exclusion are exacerbated; FSA (2000, ch. 5) devotes a chapter to the many consequences of financial exclusion.

Recent research by Kempson and Whyley (1999a) found that people without access to financial products were concerned with two broad financial services' 'gaps' (that is, unmet financial services needs): day-to-day money management and long-term financial security. Medium-term security (like household contents insurance and insurance for loss of income) was judged of lower importance. In this same survey, few respondents expressed a need for consumer credit or savings products; interestingly, there was 'considerable resistance to consumer credit *per se.*'

Not having a bank chequing account means that a household has to deal entirely in cash; this makes money management more complex, costly, less secure and time consuming. These same kinds of problems can also apply to those with a basic bank or building society account, but are still unable to access additional facilities like direct debits, overdrafts and debit and credit cards.

Exclusion from banking facilities is a particularly fundamental problem. Financially excluded households generally identify as a top priority the need for an account to receive income and make payments (FSA, 2000, para 5.3). There are three main areas of peoples' lives that are affected by not having basic banking facilities (FSA, 2000, para 5.2):

- handling cash and cheques;
- paying bills;

- and access to short-term credit facilities and other financial products that are predicated on the applicant having a banking facility.

In general, households' costs, inconvenience and efficiency in making financial transactions are all compromised in these areas without a basic banking facility. It can be very difficult, for example, to receive income and make payments without a bank account. Lack of such a facility to receive wages from an employer can also impact negatively on getting a job. Not having a bank account can also preclude a person from accessing many other financial products and services, like short-term credit and several kinds of insurance policies.

Some credit products (like overdrafts and credit cards) are generally used to smooth the peaks and troughs in household budgets and others (like hire purchase and personal loans) are used to buy goods like cars and consumer durables. People who are unable to access these kinds of credit facilities typically fall into two groups: those with a poor or non-existent credit history and people living on a low income. Both of these groups are especially vulnerable and invariably have to borrow from operators outside of mainstream financial services. Two major problems are the higher borrowing costs and the consequences of non-repayment when such loans are typically secured on the borrower's assets.

Private insurance is used nowadays to protect individuals against a widening spectrum of risks. Financial exclusion problems in this area are likely to widen as newer kinds of insurance (like health and long-term care insurance) become more common. Financial exclusion from basic insurance cover exacerbates wider social exclusion. This is because the societal groups thus excluded are often those same individuals who are most vulnerable to the risks covered. This kind of exclusion is likely to become more serious as present state welfare reforms put a greater onus on the private sector to increase its dependence on private insurance and provision.

An obvious 'cost' of financial exclusion from insurance is the increased anxiety placed on households and individuals. Typically, these are the most vulnerable groups in society and live in areas and under social conditions where many risks (like theft, property damage and health) are higher. Where such a risk is experienced and there is no respective insurance cover, the range of options is likely to be limited. For example, they may have to rely on the state if the main breadwinner in a household falls ill or dies. Another option is seeking other (typically more expensive and risky in the event of default) kinds

Table 3.3   Numbers of financial products by socio-economic circumstances (cont'd)

							row percentages
			Number of financial products[a]				
	None	*Low*	*Medium-Low*	*Average*	*Medium-High*	*High*	*Weighted Base*
	%	%	%	%	%	%	
Standard region							
North, including Cumbria	9	25	22	13	19	13	1,619
Yorkshire and Humberside	6	21	22	11	20	20	2,305
North West	9	21	20	12	20	19	2,921
East Midlands	5	19	19	12	22	23	1,926
West Midlands	6	20	20	11	21	22	2,407
East Anglia	4	17	19	12	25	23	1,067
Greater London	9	23	20	10	19	19	2,961
South East (excluding London)	3	14	17	11	24	32	5,119
South West	4	17	20	11	23	27	2,297
Scotland	13	25	19	10	19	15	2,358
Wales	8	23	25	12	18	14	1,455
Local levels of deprivation[b]							
I (most deprived)	11	27	20	11	16	15	*5,699*
2	7	23	23	11	21	16	*3,931*
3	5	19	21	13	24	20	*2,406*
4	4	15	20	13	23	25	*2,440*
5	4	13	18	11	23	31	*2,416*
6	2	13	16	11	24	34	*2,157*
7 (least deprived)	2	13	17	11	24	34	*3,573*

a   Low: I or 2 products; Medium-Low: 3 or 4 products; Average: 5 products; Medium-high: 6 or 7 products; High: 8 or more products.
b   Analysis based on the Department of the Environment, Transport and Regions (DETR) *Deprivation Index* and restricted to England and Wales.
 HoH: Head of Household
Base: all households 22,622
Source: FSA (2000, Table 3.1)

informal methods. ROSCA's (Rotating Savings and Credit Schemes) and credit unions appear to be more prominent amongst minority ethnic communities (FSA, 2000, paras 3.69 and 3.70).

Insurance access has been prominent in financial exclusion research: see, for example, (Kempson & Whyley [1999b], FSA [2000], and Sinclair [2001]). The numbers of UK households without particular

Table 3.4   **Numbers of financial products by household circumstances**

			Number of financial products[a]				*row percentages*
	None	*Low*	*Medium-Low*	*Average-High*	*Medium*	*High*	*Weighted Base*
	%	%	%	%	%	%	
All households	7	19	20	11	21	22	26,435
Net weekly household income							
No income	2	18	17	13	22	27	*179*
£1–50	6	26	28	13	18	9	*321*
£51–100	16	39	29	6	8	3	*2,785*
£101–150	16	37	26	10	9	4	*4,490*
£151–200	9	29	25	13	17	8	*3,665*
£201–300	4	15	22	16	26	18	*5,279*
£301–400	–	6	16	12	34	32	*3,631*
£400–500	–	3	8	10	31	48	*2,276*
more than £500	–	1	6	7	26	60	*3,193*
Net equivalent weekly household income							
No income	2	18	17	13	22	27	*179*
£1–50	4	19	24	16	23	14	*213*
£51–100	8	28	32	9	16	7	*191*
£101–150	15	35	29	9	9	4	*4,058*
£151–200	13	34	23	10	13	6	*5,282*
£201–300	4	17	22	14	25	19	*6,769*
£301–400	1	7	14	12	32	35	*3,976*
£400–500	–	3	10	11	30	47	*2,127*
more than £500	–	2	6	8	25	59	*2,433*
Receipt of income-related benefit							
None	–	8	20	14	28	31	*18,289*
Council Tax Benefit only	2	24	39	13	15	6	*1,229*
Income Support only	4	18	27	13	21	18	*589*
Council Tax Benefit & Income Support	3	32	40	13	9	3	*974*
Housing Benefit only	13	62	21	2	2	–	*484*
Housing Benefit & Council Tax Benefit	21	58	17	3	1	–	*1,403*
Housing Benefit & Income Support	36	49	9	2	3	2	*365*
Housing Benefit, Council Tax Benefit & Income Support	35	55	9	–	–	–	*3.102*

Table 3.4   Numbers of financial products by household circumstances
(cont'd)

							row percentages
			Number of financial products[a]				
	None	*Low*	*Medium-Low*	*Average-High*	*Medium*	*High*	*Weighted Base*
	%	*%*	*%*	*%*	*%*	*%*	
Economic activity status (HoH)							
Self employed	–	6	16	12	29	37	*2,386*
Full-time employment	–	9	16	12	29	34	*10,981*
Part-time employment	6	29	22	12	17	15	*442*
Unemployed	19	38	20	8	9	7	*1,565*
Retired	8	29	28	11	14	9	*7,262*
Sick/disabled	19	32	22	10	11	7	*1,573*
Student	8	40	28	8	10	6	*274*
Other inactive	22	32	14	6	12	14	*1,951*
No. of years since last worked (HoH)							
0	–	9	16	12	29	34	*13,809*
1	8	31	22	12	15	13	*832*
2	10	29	23	11	15	13	*810*
3	13	25	22	11	13	16	*739*
4	13	29	22	10	14	11	*782*
5	10	31	23	10	14	11	*714*
6–10	13	27	25	11	14	11	*2,455*
11–16	12	32	27	10	12	7	*3,620*
21 or more	16	39	25	8	9	4	*1,906*

a   Low: 1 or 2 products; Medium-Low: 3 or 4 products; Average: 5 products; Medium-high:
    6 or 7 products; High: 8 or more products.
    HoH: Head of Household.
Base: all *households 22,622.*
Source: FSA (2000, Table 3.2)

types of insurance (from a 1998 survey) were as follows (FSA, 2000,
para 3.73):

- 26 per cent had no home contents insurance;
- 87 per cent no mortgage payment protection insurance (MPPI);
- 91 per cent no medical insurance;
- and 93 per cent no personal accident insurance.

The characteristics of those without insurance vary according to the
kind of insurance involved. Generally, though, those who are most

likely to claim on a particular policy are correspondingly most likely to be excluded.

Direct exclusion from insurance is rare; affordability is the most important factor in explaining lack of insurance. More risk-sensitive pricing of insurance products has meant that cover is more expensive for more risky groups. Another factor is that insurance may be unaffordable to some groups because of the kind of insurance policy available. An example would be a home contents policy with a minimum level of cover that exceeds the cover required. Another important factor is that people with low incomes usually cannot pay for insurance in a way that matches their budget. For example, paying an annual premium may be too onerous and using a monthly direct debit is not feasible without a basic account as well. Other factors explaining lack of insurance include the conditions attached to policies and/or a lack of knowledge about what is available on the market.

The UK Treasury estimates that around 27 per cent of all employees are neither members of occupational pension schemes nor have personal pensions (FSA, 2000, para 3.96). The reasons for not having a private pension or making inadequate pension provision include lack of opportunity, lack of interest, lack of disposable income, lack of knowledge and mistrust of pension providers, and religious and cultural factors are important for some ethnic minorities (FSA, 2000, para 3.105).

Access to credit is often perceived to be central to the financial exclusion debate. One reason for this concern is that borrowing (whilst often necessary) invariably exacerbates the problems that low-income groups face. Indeed, the impact of credit is pervasive in the sense that credit use and 'misuse' impacts on all groups that access financial services. In the wider context of financial exclusion, some groups with access to financial services are excluded (via credit scoring, bank customer segmentation strategies etc.) from various kinds and levels of credit. Nevertheless, the use of credit has grown strongly and is now the norm. Only a relatively small proportion (though apparently growing) is without access to any form of credit. Nevertheless, those excluded from mainstream financial services are often forced to seek more expensive sources, (like money lenders, pawnbrokers, mail order catalogues and cheque cashers).

There has been a marked growth in both the volume and different kinds of credit available in the UK market during recent years. High rates of financial innovation, intense competition, aggressive marketing, greater sophistication in credit risk appraisal, the pursuit of customer segmentation strategies, greater sophistication in risk-based pricing and more emphasis on shareholder value maximisation in FSF strategies are some of the key features of the UK mass market in credit. As we saw earlier, these developments have apparently exacerbated the polarisation of access to financial services.

Compared with other kinds of financial services, there are much higher rates of 'denied access' to mainstream credit (FSA, 2000, para 3.137). People are unable to access mainstream financial services for many reasons. Non-status borrowers (who have a poor or non-existent credit history), for example, are unable to obtain mainstream credit facilities. These borrowers are also often 'encouraged' to pursue non-status borrowing via less strict lending criteria of non-mainstream lenders, extensive media advertising and lack of knowledge of alternatives. Mainstream lenders may also be unable to meet their needs. These borrowers are typically seeking small sums of money for relatively short periods of time.

Barriers to financial inclusion

It is clear that different 'groups' of people may be unable to access particular kinds of financial products for many reasons. There is no single factor that explains financial exclusion and no unique solution is feasible for all kinds of exclusion. It is also the case that even in relatively deprived and isolated communities, outright refusal to provide services by financial institutions is rare.

Nevertheless, until quite recently, financial institutions have not expended great efforts to help service economically vulnerable and marginalised groups (Sinclair, 2001, Section 7). A basic problem is often the mismatch between the products on offer and potential customers' needs (HM Treasury, 1999, p. 1).

FSA (2000, p. 46) identifies various kinds of barriers to inclusion within the financial services sector. These include the following:

- access difficulties
- lack of appropriate financial products
- affordability
- lack of appropriate delivery mechanisms
- poor levels of knowledge
- psychological barriers, including a mistrust of suppliers
- language and cultural problems
- the impact of legislation and regulation

These barriers do not apply to all financial products and, where they do, they can differ considerably in their nature and impact.

There are many different kinds of access barrier, including geographical access, access for those with disabilities, risk assessment, racism and marketing. Geographic (or physical) access has been restricted in poorer communities where the level of basic branch provision is comparatively low. It is also the case that those societal groups that are especially prone to financial exclusion are also those that find it more difficult to get to a more remote bank branch. These groups are also more resistant to cash machines or ATMs and have less access to them: see, for example Kempson and Jones (2000) and Thrift and Leyshon (1997). These same groups often feel more comfortable using a building society or Post Office. Many small local building societies are also reluctant to close branches and are more committed to their local community (FSA, 2000, p. 46). This 'regional identity' (with an associated greater knowledge and strategic concern with regional development) is a feature of traditional UK building societies.

Geographic access has also been affected by cost cutting pressures in the insurance sector. One such area is the method of selling insurance directly to householders via a salesman calling at each home; the same technique was also used to collect premiums. Lower income families and other societal groups (like those with physical disabilities) were better able to access basic insurance services through these means. However, many companies no longer use this mode of service delivery.

Many physical disabilities comprise barriers to inclusion. These vary from mobility through to sight, hearing and other impediments. As a result, people with these kinds of disabilities may be unable to read ATM screens or use telephone-based services.

Risk assessment, as we discussed earlier, is another area that can provide a barrier to financial services. On the one hand, more accurate risk analysis and related pricing have increased inclusion; financial products can be tailored and priced on a more accurate economic basis so as to make them available to a wider clientele. On the downside, though, more accurate and detailed risk screening operates by definition against those groups who are more 'risky' in a credit scoring context: like low income groups, people living in deprived neighbourhoods and those with a history of poor payment. The impact of modern risk assessment methods varies between different kinds of financial product. For example, the impact of risk assessment is more evident in consumer credit, whilst 'affordability' is more relevant to insurance access (FSA, 2000, pp. 47–48).

More focussed marketing and greater sophistication in segmenting customers can also exacerbate exclusion. Modern marketing techniques and associated customer (actual and potential) information data files allow FSFs to target much more selectively. The result is that those at the margins of inclusion are unlikely to be targeted for promotional literature of new and existing financial products. As a result, a growing asymmetric information gap develops between those excluded and financial product providers (Leyshon *et al*, 1998).

Racism is another apparent barrier. There is evidence that some financial service staff may discriminate against ethnic minority groups (FSA, 2000, para 4.17). Nevertheless, no clear evidence supports the allegation that banks and other credit firms are racist in their credit granting.

Within the financial services industry, there have been periodic 'flights to quality'. These have increased the banking importance of more accurate credit screening and avoiding clusters of customers who are 'financially fragile'. One result has been the development of a wider range of more tailored and sophisticated products for profitable customer groups. As a result, the gap between the financially included (supplied with a greater variety of new products than ever before) and those excluded (increasingly discriminated against on the basis of their credit risk potential) widens. The same product innovation effort expended on wealthier customer groups is not devoted towards the design, testing and delivery of more appropriate products for lower income and other excluded groups.

Many products developed for lower income groups have since been withdrawn. These include, for example, indemnity home contents insurance that allows cover for second-hand replacements of damaged or stolen possessions and budgeting accounts that allow individuals to spread costs. Another such 'product gap' is borrowing for short periods with a weekly (and sometimes varying) pattern of repayments. Relatively large deposits may also be needed to open new savings accounts. Although many low income groups save regularly via life insurance, there is widespread agreement that this is not a suitable kind of savings product for those with a low and/or fluctuating income stream (FSA, 2000, para 4.23). Lack of transparency and inflexibility are also factors that are important in not taking out a private pension. Several studies have also drawn attention to a lack of financial products that accord with Islamic requirements (HM Treasury, 1999).

Affordability is a serious barrier. Those with low incomes face a corresponding reduced ability to access any but the most basic and cheapest of financial products. At the same time, low income groups often have to pay more because of their lower credit standing. This 'double-edged sword' can be a major barrier. Another aspect is the reduced ability of those without a bank account to spread the costs of home contents insurance (FSA, 2000, para 4.29).

Methods of service delivery can also be important (Joseph Rowntree Foundation, 1999). Sinclair (2001, Section 7.9) suggests that telephone banking is obviously of little use to those without a telephone! The BBA (2003, p. 6) points out that of the 12,000 or so retail bank branches in the UK, over 1,000 provide customers with access to the Internet. Nevertheless, the rise of Internet banking will also discriminate against those households without a PC or access to one. Generation attitudes (the older generation prefer more overt means of banking) and technology-literacy may also be relevant barriers in this context.

Financial literacy has several aspects. Research shows that consumers often do not have the information and/or expertise to make informed decisions about purchasing financial products. Even more sophisticated included groups are often 'challenged' in choosing amongst the many financial options offered to them. This problem is exacerbated for those on the margin of mainstream financial services; not only may they lack basic financial literacy, but they also may be unaware of even viable (for them) products available. Research has shown that financial literacy and exclusion often begin in early childhood: see FSA (2000, para 4.31) and FSA (2000a).

Psychological barriers and mistrust of suppliers can also be effective barriers. Lack of knowledge is often associated with generalised mistrust of financial services firms by those on the periphery of mainstream financial services. Banks are often seen as being uninterested in those with low incomes, although building societies are often viewed as more helpful. Many people on low incomes save through informal means. Insurance companies probably have the most negative image (FSA, 2000, para 4.36). The publicity surrounding the mis-selling of pensions and endowment policies increased the distrust of financial services providers. The perceived inadequate response by UK regulators to these scandals has not helped to mitigate this distrust.

Language and cultural barriers also appear to be significant, especially for those from Pakistani and Bangladeshi communities (FSA, 2000, para 4.38). These barriers appear strongest for first generation immigrants.

Finally, the impact of Government policy and regulation can lead to barriers. We saw earlier, for example, that money laundering regulations have had the unintended effect of restricting access to banking. The regulation of savings and investment product selling and social security regulations on means testing have restricted access to financial products. The system of social security benefits payable in cash has helped to encourage recipients to remain unbanked. Without a basic banking facility, other financial products are invariably less easily accessed.

Consequences of financial exclusion

There are many consequences of financial exclusion. Although, on balance a higher proportion of the UK population is now financially included compared with earlier times, we have seen that apparent polarisation of the financially excluded has increased. At the same time, the consequences of not being able to access basic financial products (bank account, consumer credit, insurance and long-term investments or a pension) are more serious when the majority of households have these products. With this kind of polarisation, the more general problems of social exclusion are exacerbated; FSA (2000, ch. 5) devotes a chapter to the many consequences of financial exclusion.

Recent research by Kempson and Whyley (1999a) found that people without access to financial products were concerned with two broad financial services' 'gaps' (that is, unmet financial services needs): day-to-day money management and long-term financial security. Medium-term security (like household contents insurance and insurance for loss of income) was judged of lower importance. In this same survey, few respondents expressed a need for consumer credit or savings products; interestingly, there was 'considerable resistance to consumer credit *per se.*'

Not having a bank chequing account means that a household has to deal entirely in cash; this makes money management more complex, costly, less secure and time consuming. These same kinds of problems can also apply to those with a basic bank or building society account, but are still unable to access additional facilities like direct debits, overdrafts and debit and credit cards.

Exclusion from banking facilities is a particularly fundamental problem. Financially excluded households generally identify as a top priority the need for an account to receive income and make payments (FSA, 2000, para 5.3). There are three main areas of peoples' lives that are affected by not having basic banking facilities (FSA, 2000, para 5.2):

• handling cash and cheques;
• paying bills;

- and access to short-term credit facilities and other financial products that are predicated on the applicant having a banking facility.

In general, households' costs, inconvenience and efficiency in making financial transactions are all compromised in these areas without a basic banking facility. It can be very difficult, for example, to receive income and make payments without a bank account. Lack of such a facility to receive wages from an employer can also impact negatively on getting a job. Not having a bank account can also preclude a person from accessing many other financial products and services, like short-term credit and several kinds of insurance policies.

Some credit products (like overdrafts and credit cards) are generally used to smooth the peaks and troughs in household budgets and others (like hire purchase and personal loans) are used to buy goods like cars and consumer durables. People who are unable to access these kinds of credit facilities typically fall into two groups: those with a poor or non-existent credit history and people living on a low income. Both of these groups are especially vulnerable and invariably have to borrow from operators outside of mainstream financial services. Two major problems are the higher borrowing costs and the consequences of non-repayment when such loans are typically secured on the borrower's assets.

Private insurance is used nowadays to protect individuals against a widening spectrum of risks. Financial exclusion problems in this area are likely to widen as newer kinds of insurance (like health and long-term care insurance) become more common. Financial exclusion from basic insurance cover exacerbates wider social exclusion. This is because the societal groups thus excluded are often those same individuals who are most vulnerable to the risks covered. This kind of exclusion is likely to become more serious as present state welfare reforms put a greater onus on the private sector to increase its dependence on private insurance and provision.

An obvious 'cost' of financial exclusion from insurance is the increased anxiety placed on households and individuals. Typically, these are the most vulnerable groups in society and live in areas and under social conditions where many risks (like theft, property damage and health) are higher. Where such a risk is experienced and there is no respective insurance cover, the range of options is likely to be limited. For example, they may have to rely on the state if the main breadwinner in a household falls ill or dies. Another option is seeking other (typically more expensive and risky in the event of default) kinds of borrowing. In many instances, financial exclusion inevitably re-inforces the wider consequences of social exclusion.

The lack of pension provision is another important area of financial exclusion. Since providing for a pension is increasingly the norm for most people, lack of pension provision further exacerbates the increasing polarisation of access to financial services. The obvious consequence of not having a pension is the increased likelihood of poverty and hardship in old age. The Joseph Rowntree Foundation (1995) found that the gap between those in the UK with private pension provision and those without is becoming more marked. Like other financially excluded groups, people without an adequate private pension face a restricted choice of options. Those unable or unwilling (for good reasons, like wishing to leave something to their children) to draw on their own savings or their property value, often choose by default greater hardship. The same applies to those who do not have such choices, where state-based support has to be the only option.

FSA (2000, para 5.50) suggests that the consequences of not having savings financial products fall into two broad groups. First, is the problem of not having any formal savings products and having to save via informal methods. Second, is the consequence of being without any savings.

The problem of not having formal savings is that people lose out *inter alia* on interest rates available and possible tax advantages. This kind of informal savings (keeping cash in the house) is also much less secure than formal savings products. The stark consequence of not having savings at all is the loss of security and flexibility that many with savings take for granted. Research has shown that being without savings is a particular cause of concern for parents, especially single parents (Kempson and Whyley, 1999a).

Financial exclusion impacts not only on the individuals and households concerned, but also on the wider communities in which they reside. Leyshon and Thrift (1994), for example, point out that the withdrawal of financial services in an area is typically associated with low economic growth, social problems and a decaying built environment. Lack of financial services in an area, for example, may deter small business start-ups and inward investment. Closing an area's only bank branch can reduce trade in local shops as residents go elsewhere for their shopping.

Leyshon and Thrift (1995) demonstrate these 'Holes that are beginning to appear in the geography of retail financial services provision...' in the UK. They point out that the financial services industry in the US and in Britain has become increasingly exclusionary in response to financial crises associated with higher levels of competition and extreme levels of indebtedness. Furthermore, the kind of uneven development associated with financially excluded 'spaces' can become entrenched because of the modern methods used to assess risk within the financial services industry (Leyshon and Thrift, 1995, p. 315). US experiences (see also the following chapter) are also interesting and relevant in this context.

We discussed this problem earlier in the context of the new kinds of risk assessment methods being used in the financial services industry. Customer 'clusters' of financial fragility (high credit risk) may become increasingly disenfranchised from mainstream financial services. One consequence is an apparent geographic clustering of financial exclusion. This and other factors lead to a situation where the richer areas become better served and more prosperous; deprived areas, in turn, become poorer and ever more disadvantaged. A kind of cycle or 'spiral' of exclusion and greater polarisation may ensue.

We have also noted, for example, that recent UK press attention (Mills, 2003) has focused on call centres picking out wealthier customers for 'special attention'; this press article was based on recent research by market analysts Datamonitor. Customers calling at the same time from the same region, but with different post codes, apparently received a 'drastically different level of service' from leading banks and other service industry firms. Banks argue that they want their most articulate staff dealing with the best customers who are typically taken through many more financial product options than poorer customers. The 'best customers' merit this treatment since they are the customers who generate the most 'value added' for the bank.

Boyce (2000) also explores this phenomenon in some detail. He makes the point that the deregulation-induced 'customer revolution' of the 1980s centred on notions like 'customer focus' and 'providing value to customers'. But these soon gave way to 'calculation of the financial value of customers to an organisation'. This shareholder-value driven imperative reconstructs the customer as an asset (or a liability), segments the customer base, and treats customers as 'profit centres' rather than people. It leads to a focus on particular customers and groups of customers (that is, the more profitable ones) rather than the customer in general. The apparent cost of this new banking strategy has been the further marginalisation of poorer and more disadvantaged people.

Modern banking theory focuses on the problems of information asymmetry. Asymmetric information between banks and their customers, existing and potential, is a source of potential risk and, of course, potential profit. In the 'old world' (pre-deregulation, pre-globalisation and before modern technological breakthroughs) this information asymmetry was tackled through closer personal, face-to-face banking transacted through branches. Technology has now facilitated data collection, processing, evaluation, storage and monitoring of customers 'at a distance'. Consumers have also had to develop new kinds of relationships of trust with retail FSFs; this is typically based on identifying with brands and the ability to process various media.

In this new world, those excluded from the financial system face a kind of 'double handicap' (Leyshon *et al*, 1998, p. 29): they live in both a financial and information 'shadow'. Leyshon *et al* (1998, p. 47) conclude:

> The changes we have outlined in the financial services industry and in the consumers of its products are leading to greater levels of uneven development which is both financial and informational, the two being clearly related.

On the one hand, the majority of consumers apparently benefit from these changes. They are able to purchase either generic and increasingly transparent financial products or more tailored services. The 'losers' are a significant minority of less-affluent customers... 'who are increasingly characterised as bad financial risks because of who they are or where they live, or both'.

Researchers appear unanimous on these apparent consequences of the 'new banking'. This is a complex issue and we will shortly explore some of the proposed solutions. One apparent problem is that this new banking may downgrade the economic importance (to the bank) of regional banking, especially the peripheral regions. All of this may appear to confirm an inherent conflict between banking 'value maximisation' and society's longer-term best interests.

Conclusions

This chapter outlines the main features of financial exclusion in the UK. We show that changes in the general economy and financial firm behaviour are having the effect of creating various groups in society who find it difficult (if not impossible) to access basic financial services. The consequences of this are straightforward – various consumers do not have the means to conduct transactions effectively, cannot obtain credit on reasonable terms or insure the few assets they have. These groups also are constrained in their ability to accumulate savings or make contributions for retirement. Financial exclusion can also exacerbate various individual's access to welfare payments that are increasingly processed through banks and other financial institutions. Financial exclusion can be viewed as a complement to wider social and political exclusion. It is therefore taken seriously by policymakers. The following chapter outlines various initiatives that have been taken by the UK Government and other bodies aimed at tackling this issue.

4
Tackling Financial Exclusion in the UK

Introduction

This chapter outlines the various approaches that have been suggested as means to tackling financial exclusion. Eradicating financial exclusion has been a major priority of the UK Government since the mid-1990's onwards and is becoming increasingly important throughout Europe and elsewhere. A range of initiatives have been developed. Unlike in the US where policy aimed at dealing with financial exclusion has been mainly through the enactment of various legislation, in the UK the policy response to date has been characterised by Government as 'facilitator and mediator', with an emphasis on a partnership approach. In this 'model', the banks and the Post Office have a key role to play in helping to overcome financial exclusion. The main features of the various policy approaches taken are discussed in this chapter.

Government and financial sector partnership

Dealing with financial exclusion has become a major priority for the UK Labour Government since the mid-1990's onwards. The UK Government established 18 PATs (Policy Action Teams) following the Social Exclusion Unit (SEU, 1998) report; PAT 14 is concerned specifically with financial exclusion. PAT 14 and the Cruickshank (2000) report comprise key parts of the policy context of the present UK Government's developing approach to dealing with financial exclusion.

It is clear that there is no single cause of financial exclusion. Who you are, where you live, personal experiences (or lack of them) with financial services, financial literacy and individual prejudices, can all exacerbate the problem. Most people without financial products are excluded through the combined effects of marketing, their own lack of financial literacy, pricing and inappropriate product structure. Although around 25 per cent of those excluded in the UK have used financial products in the past, the majority excluded have never used financial products at all. Some of these excluded (a relatively small group) have either been refused financial products or have consciously decided not to access them. Although some people experience short periods of financial exclusion, for others it can be longer term (even life-long).

Financial exclusion, then, is a complex, dynamic and apparently sustainable process: exclusion from basic products means that access to other kinds of financial services becomes even more difficult. As we have seen, there are many barriers to financial exclusion and a variety of damaging consequences. 'Free market solutions' unaided do not appear to be capable of tackling this problem.

In the UK there is a strong commitment from both Government and the financial services industry to seek and deploy appropriate ways of tackling financial exclusion. The Governor of the Bank of England has urged the big banks to tackle the problem of financial exclusion (Trenor, 1999). The Cruickshank Inquiry (2000) was concerned about the issue of financial inclusion and how it might be mitigated.

It is clear that FSFs have an important role to play in overcoming financial exclusion; there also appears to be a general consensus that they cannot do this by themselves. Financial services firms are guided mainly by commercial considerations and overcoming financial exclusion is unlikely to be achieved primarily on commercial grounds, at least in the foreseeable short term.

In the UK there is a strong consensus that partnerships offer the best route for tackling financial exclusion (FSA, 2000, para 7.3). These kinds of partnerships involve central government, regulators, local authorities, other commercial organisations and not-for-profit organisations. Whilst these partnerships are particularly important for tackling access problems, they are also seen to have a key role in tackling financial literacy and helping to reduce the psychological barriers of many who are financially excluded. The financial services industry is important in the key area of appropriate product design. Government has an important role to play as facilitator, mediator and regulator.

We saw earlier that there are many aspects of increasing access to financial services. The FSA (2000, para 7.5) summarises these as geographical access, access for those with disabilities, risk assessment and alleged racism.

Most providers committed to overcoming financial exclusion believe that widening geographical access can only be achieved through the partnership route. Even without bank and building society branch closures, there still remain many who are distanced from a branch because they live in a new or growing community. Financial services firms are unlikely to accord high priority to poorer localities. Instead, they are looking to technology and partnerships with other organisations to expand geographic access. Kempson and Jones (2000) point out however, that technology is unlikely to improve access for those who are at the margin of financial services since they seek more control over their own finances than these new forms of banking provide.

Supermarkets were seen initially as one 'partnership' (private/private) route to help reduce financial exclusion (Kempson, 1994). However, reality does not appear to bear out these initial hopes. Alexander and Pollard (2000), for example, argue that the entry of grocery retailers into financial services in the UK raises some important issues and confirms that these moves have not generally increased access to financial services for those excluded. In practice, they have targeted wealthier customers who are likely to buy a range of profitable financial products.

The Post Office is seen as a promising key initiative for increasing access to financial services; there are many reasons for this view. The Post Office has over 19,000 outlets and these cover every deprived community in the UK and many small rural areas. People who do not have a bank or building society account still use the Post Office for many financial transactions, including encashment of pensions or state benefits and paying bills by postal orders (instead of cheques).

Post Office Counters Limited (POCL) also faces a significant loss of income starting (via a phased process) in 2003 when pensions and benefits became paid electronically by ACT (Automated Credit Transfer) into accounts. One of the main strands of PO policy in the future is to expand its role in providing financial services. Unlike the supermarkets, it will almost certainly be directly concerned with meeting the banking needs of those who are currently financially excluded.

In the March 2000 budget statement, the Chancellor of the Exchequer called on the banks and the Post Office to offer a 'basic banking service to all' in order to help tackle the problem of financial exclusion. The Government is demanding a universal banking service to help tackle financial exclusion. In this context, talks accelerated between the banks and the Post Office to provide a basic banking service to everyone in society.

UK retail banks have formed a kind of partnership with the UK Government under the umbrella of the BBA (British Bankers Association) to help tackle financial exclusion. Like Government, the banking industry is committed to the objective that every citizen should have access to financial services.

From 2000, the BBA has published an annual report on the promotion of financial inclusion. In their first report, they emphasise (2000, p. 4) that there has been a substantial growth in financial inclusion during recent years: only around 6–9 per cent of the population (about 3 million) do not now have a bank account. In their first report, they identify (2000, p. 3) a number of key areas for particular attention in the UK:

- Developing basic bank accounts;
- Working with the Financial Services Authority (FSA) on money laundering rules so that financial exclusion is not exacerbated;
- The promotion of financial literacy and partnership between banks and other organisations so that awareness of basic bank accounts is increased and their utility made more transparent;
- Helping all societal groups to benefit from new and developing delivery channels;
- Encouraging partnerships between the credit union movement and the banks;
- Working with all credit granting organisations to improve access to free, independent money advice;
- Promoting the development of micro credit systems and promulgating good practice in these schemes.

This 'agenda' summarised the (then) UK banking sector response to strong government pressure to tackle financial exclusion. Pollin and Riva (in Ruozi and Anderloni, 2002, p. 230) describe this UK 'model' as 'Government as a Mediator'.

Universal banking and basic banking services

In its reform of social security payments (from Spring 2003 all welfare benefits and tax credits became paid through the banking system), the UK Government called on the banks and the Post Office to offer a 'basic banking service'. Government put pressure on the banks to supply their own basic bank account and to make these accounts available via the Post Office's branches. Government supports strongly the idea of a 'universal banking service' provided via the Post Office in a formal public-private partnership: the Post Office providing delivery facilities and wider geographic access, with the High Street banks sharing the costs.

Basic bank accounts are designed to provide customers with both easy access to their money and a convenient vehicle for undertaking electronic transactions. The basic features of current basic bank accounts (BBA, 2002, p. 8) are as follows:

- Wages, salaries, pensions, benefits etc can be paid by ACT;
- Cheques and cash can be paid into the account;
- Cash can be withdrawn from cash machines;
- Bills can be paid by direct debit, or standing order, or by transferring money to another account.

Basic bank accounts (sometimes called starter accounts or introductory accounts) are seen as one of the key ways of promoting financial inclusion. Most basic bank accounts were introduced (following Government encouragement) in October, 2000. By the end of 2001, three and a half million basic bank accounts had been opened (Mullen, 2001, p. 4). Table 4.1 summarises some of the key features of these basic banking services.

The basic bank account is closely associated with the 'universal bank' initiative. There is no physical universal bank; it is more a 'generic model' based on the Post Office. The essence of 'universal banking services' comprises two aspects:

- Initially 12 banks and building societies agreed to make their basic bank accounts available free at Post Office counters from April 2003. The initially participating institutions were: Abbey National, Alliance & Leicester, Bank of Ireland, Barclays, First Trust Bank, HBOS, HSBC, Lloyds TSB, National Australia Group, Nationwide, The Co-operative Bank and the Royal Bank of Scotland Group.
- The Post Office introduced (in May, 2001) a Post Office card account, the Clear Account. This is a very simple account for receiving benefits, pensions and tax credit payments and cash withdrawals at the Post Office counters.

From April 2003, basic bank account-holders were able to draw cash without charge at Post Office branches. Of the 6.15 million basic bank

Table 4.1 The basic bank accounts of British banks

Bank name and name of account	Cash withdrawal is available at the Post Office	Minimum age to open account	Minimum amount to open account	Automated Credit Transfer (ACT) payments[1]	Cash machine card	Free buffer zone[2]	Direct Debits and Standing Orders	Charge for unpaid Direct Debit[3]	Debit card (Solo or Electron)	Cheque book
Abbey National Basic Current Account	Yes	16	None	Yes	Yes	£10	Yes	£32	No	No
Alliance & Leicester Basic Banking Account	Yes	18	None	Yes	Yes	No	Yes	£29.50	No	No
Bank of Ireland Basic Cash Account	Yes	16	None	Yes	Yes	No	Yes	£38	No	No
Bank of Scotland Easycash[5]	Yes	16	None	Yes	Yes	No	Yes	£30	No	No
Barclays Cash Card Account	Yes	18	None	Yes	Yes	No	Direct Debits only	£30 max per account per day	No	No
Clydesdale Cashmaster	Yes	16	None	Yes	Yes	No	Yes	£33	No	No
Co-operative Bank Cashminder	Yes	16	None	Yes	Yes	No	Yes	No	Yes	No

Table 4.1 The basic bank accounts of British banks (*continued*)

Bank name and name of account	Cash withdrawal is available at the Post Office	Minimum age to open account	Minimum amount to open account	Automated Credit Transfer (ACT) payments[1]	Cash machine card	Free buffer zone[2]	Direct Debits and Standing Orders	Charge for unpaid Direct Debit[3]	Debit card (Solo or Electron)	Cheque book
First Trust Bank Basic Bank Account	Yes	16	None	Yes	Yes	£10	Direct Debits only	Under £35– £22.50[6] Over £35– £37.50	No	No
Halifax Easycash	Yes	16	None	Yes	Yes	No	Yes	£30	No	No
HSBC Basic Bank Account	Yes	18	None	Yes	Yes	£10	Yes	No	No	No
Lloyds TSB Basic Bank Account	Yes	18[4]	None	Yes	Yes	£10	Yes	No	No	No
Nationwide Building Society FlexAccount Cash Card	Yes	16	£1	Yes	Yes	No	Yes	£25 (£27.50 from 1st June)	No	No

Table 4.1 The basic bank accounts of British banks (continued)

Bank name and name of account	Cash withdrawal is available at the Post Office	Minimum age to open account	Minimum amount to open account	Automated Credit Transfer (ACT) payments[1]	Cash machine card	Free buffer zone[2]	Direct Debits and Standing Orders	Charge for unpaid Direct Debit[3]	Debit card (Solo or Electron)	Cheque book
NatWest Step Account	Yes	16	None	Yes	Yes	No	Yes	£30	Yes	No
Northern Bank Cashmaster – Basic	Yes	16	None	Yes	Yes	No	Yes	£38	No	No
The Royal Bank of Scotland Key Account	Yes	16	None	Yes	Yes	No	Yes	£30	No	No
Ulster Bank Basic Bank Account	Yes	16	None	Yes	Yes	No	Yes	Under £20–£35 Over £20–£37.50	No	No
Yorkshire Bank Readycash	Yes	16	None	Yes	Yes	No	Yes	£33	No	No

Table 4.1 The basic bank accounts of British banks (*continued*)

Bank name and name of account	Cash withdrawal is available at the Post Office	Minimum age to open account	Minimum amount to open account	Automated Credit Transfer (ACT) payments[1]	Cash machine card	Free buffer zone[2]	Direct Debits and Standing Orders	Charge for unpaid Direct Debit[3]	Debit card (Solo or Electron)	Cheque book
Post Office Card Account Post Office card account is offered by Citibank International Plc through Post Office Ltd	Yes	None	None	Yes[7]	No	No	No	N/A	No	No

Notes: If an individual is un-discharged bankrupt or has a record of fraud they may be prevented from obtaining these accounts
1. People who pay regularly can use Automated Credit Transfer (ACT) to pay money directly into bank accounts, instead of by cash and cheque.
2. A free temporary overdraft, so money can be taken from a cash machine if there is less than £10 in the account.
3. Correct at time of publication
4. 16-year-olds can open a similar account
5. Bank of Scotland Easycash accounts opened prior to April 2003 have different account features
6. Reserve the right to change
7. The only Automated Credit Transfer (ACT) that can be made into the card account are benefits, state pensions and some tax credits.
Source: Adapted from FSA (2003) p. 8

accounts at September 2003, 1.24 million were accessible at the Post Office (compared with 1.09 million at end-June, 2003): see BBA (23 December, 2003). In December, 2003, 16 banks offered basic accounts that were accessible via Post Office branches. 126,078 new accounts (net of closures) were opened in the quarter ended 30 September, 2003 and 11,208 basic bank accounts upgraded.

Up-to-date statistics on the current availability of basic bank accounts, together with their key features, are posted on the BBA website at www.bba.org.uk/consumers. The UK banking industry has pledged in excess of £180 million of funding over five years for the Universal Bank. The LINK (the biggest ATM switch in the world) network is now handling electronic banking transactions between 17,000 Post Offices and participating banks and building societies.

The UK Government is strongly committed to the Universal Bank initiative, but there have been criticisms. For example, the NCC (National Consumer Council) criticised the initiative as expensive, ill-considered and duplicating activities covered elsewhere: see Sinclair (2001, Section 10.4). The NCC believes that the costs of this initiative will fall largely on the commercial banks and building societies, and might compromise their European and global competitiveness.

Sinclair (2001) draws attention to the NCC questioning of the principle that, 'banks and other private sector institutions have social obligations which extend to offering cheaper, cross-subsidised services to lower income groups...' The NCC appear to favour the Cruickshank review of competition (published in March, 2000) view that government should 'define a universal service obligation and then tender for the lowest subsidy required to deliver that service'. This approach treats basic banking as a public good, rather than via cross-subsidies by bank customers that may distract competition (Sinclair, 2001, Section 10.4).

Nevertheless, the basic banking services initiative appears to have been successful to date on present showing. There is also an apparent general view that the Post Office has an important role to play in tackling financial exclusion. The FSA (2000, para 7.11) points out in this connection: 'Not only will it increase access to financial services, but it will safeguard local post offices, and the shops in which many are based, in communities that, otherwise, have very few services within them'. There are still some reservations though, as we have seen. Another concern is that the Post Office could become a monopoly supplier in some communities.

Promoting financial literacy and closing the information gap

An important aspect of universal banking and combating financial exclusion is that of promoting financial literacy. Sinclair (2001, Section 9.6) points out that 'knowledge and awareness of financial products is remarkably low among marginalised and excluded households'. Enhancing financial services awareness and literacy is widely regarded as an important component of responding to financial exclusion. UK research suggests that improving levels of financial literacy is a major factor in tackling financial exclusion (BBA, 2002, p. 15). Alongside providing appropriate delivery channels and products more suited to the needs of excluded groups, awareness of these products and knowledge of how to access and use them are often a serious problem. Psychological barriers may also be prevalent when financial awareness and literacy are comparatively low. There is distrust and disbelief that the financial services industry is concerned with these excluded groups.

These kinds of concerns have prompted many calls for better information, more widely disseminated, targeted at excluded and marginalised groups, provided by a credible and unbiased source, and provided free. The FSA has a remit to improve consumer information, advice and education (FSA, 2001, para 7.6).

The BBA (2002, p. 15) argues that improving financial literacy is both a key component of tackling financial exclusion and also… 'the biggest challenge'. Like many other challenges in improving financial inclusion, it can only be met effectively by partnership approaches. Major UK banks appear to be committed to several financial literacy projects (BBA, 2002, p. 15).

The problems of financial literacy are compounded by national school curricula and social background. Children from poor family backgrounds are unlikely to see or experience in any meaningful way how financial services can be deployed. The education system up until recently has not handled financial literacy. Although financial literacy is now part of the Citizenship component of the National Curriculum, it is still not compulsory. Teachers also do not have all the specific skills to cover these basic needs and they invariably have to meet more immediate curricula priorities.

Nevertheless, changes in UK schools curricula since 2000 have meant that children from the age of five are taught personal finance education (Clarke, 2004). Financial literacy is also taught to pupils under 14 via personal, social and health education (PSHE). From 2005, financial literacy skills will be further developed when every UK pupil will be entitled to at least five days enterprise education. At the sixth form level (schooling for 16 to 18 year olds) the Institute of Financial Services (IFS) has introduced a new qualification, the Certificate in Financial Studies, through which students can gain points towards university entry.

Another organisation known as the Personal Finance Education Group (PFEG) has been set up to 'promote and facilitate the education of all UK school pupils about their personal finances and long-term security'. The work of PFEG is supported by the BBA and a number of banks (BBA, 2002, p. 16). PFEG, for example, publicises through its website (www.pfeg.org.uk) curricula material for use by teachers. In November 2001 PFEG launched its 'Excellence and Access' project, which is designed to help teachers become more skilled and confident in teaching personal finance. The inauguration of the HM Treasury Child Trust Fund will increase the pressure and apparent need to improve financial education in schools and generally.

Adult financial literacy is being tackled in many ways. BBA has worked with the Basic Skills Agency on two projects:

• compiling curriculum materials on financial literacy to be used in citizens' advice burcaux and other respected intermediaries; and
• piloting training for financial services staff.

These two projects have been completed and the training and materials disseminated.

The UK Government has invested heavily in improving financial literacy skills of adults who have been 'failed' in this regard by the education system (Clarke, 2004, pp. 6 & 7). Such schemes include training programmes like 'Financial Skills for Life' and the 'Community Finance and Learning Initiative' (managed by the Basic Skills Agency). The AdFlag Adult Literary Financial Advisory Group (AdFlag) was established by the Department for Education and Employment, following a call from the Secretary of State for Education and Employment for a joint venture between the Government and the financial services sector to 'change dramatically advice and help on money management and family budgeting'.

BBA (2002) discusses several projects and approaches towards improving financial literacy in the UK. Training materials and videos are appearing and being used to teach adult financial literacy at credit unions, Citizens' Advice Bureaux (CABx) and money advice centres.

Partnership arrangements appear to be growing in importance. Two such initiatives are the Community and Learning Finance Initiative (CLFI), piloted by the Department for Education and Skills (DfES), and the FSA-sponsored Adult Financial Capability Framework. Although a great deal of good work is being done in these areas, it is often fragmented and not well co-ordinated with other projects. BBA (2002, p. 23) reports a strong need and impetus for national-level co-ordination of all this work.

Money and financial advice are other key aspects of financial literacy and more general financial communication between the financial services industry and its customers, both existing and potential. Furthermore, the financial services industry and its regulators have come in for considerable criticism on scandals like pensions mis-selling, split capital investment trusts and endowment-linked mortgage policies. These kinds of events have prompted regulatory responses, but they have done nothing to alleviate psychological barriers fuelled by a distrust of the financial services industry.

Consumers' concerns about advice and information on financial services were surveyed and reported by the National Consumer Council in 1999. They drew attention (NCC, p. 3) to the continued widespread use of commission in selling financial services that acts as a barrier to disinterested and objective advice. Although product choice and availability has widened, this proliferation has added to the potential for confusion.

Table 4.2 from this survey summarises consumers' view about the seven most important factors for an effective financial advice service. People in different socio-economic groups ranked these factors differently. For example, in the lowest socio-economic group, classified as DE 'a clear explanation of everything I don't understand' was valued as most important (40%), whilst 'free advice' came next (21%).

Consumers were also asked about the extent to which they agreed or disagreed with five statements abut financial information and advice. Table 4.3 compares the views of people who have not made financial decisions in the past five years with those who have. Table 4.4 provides some comparative data: 1994 NCC survey findings are compared with 1999. In both of these surveys, most respondents believe that it is difficult to get truly independent advice on financial services. Despite some positive changes (1999 compared with 1994), it is clear that the industry still has some considerable work to do.

The UK banking industry supports free money advice agencies like the Citizen's Advice Bureaux (CABx), National Debtline, Consumer

Table 4.2 Seven most important factors for an effective financial advice service – details of cumulative responses

Which would be the most important to you if you were choosing a financial advice service?

%

	Explain everything	Take account of overall situation	Free advice	No jargon	Clear figures about costs	Face-to-face contact	Independent body/ information	None/Don't know
All	40	26	18	17	16	16	14	24
Sex								
Male	40	27	18	18	18	17	18	19
Female	40	25	17	16	15	14	10	28
Age Group								
16–24	39	25	21	22	14	13	11	24
25–34	37	32	17	19	20	14	15	21
35–44	41	32	13	15	22	11	19	15
45–54	46	26	16	18	18	16	18	18
55–64	41	25	19	15	12	23	14	21
65–74	43	17	24	14	11	19	6	34
75+	29	13	17	16	11	14	4	54
Social Group								
AB	35	29	11	13	21	13	20	23
C1	40	29	16	17	18	14	18	19
C2	44	30	21	19	15	18	12	20
DE	40	19	21	19	13	17	8	32

Table 4.2 Seven most important factors for an effective financial advice service – details of cumulative responses *(continued)*

Which would be the most important to you if you were choosing a financial advice service?

	Explain everything	Take account of overall situation	Free advice	No jargon	Clear figures about costs	Face-to-face contact	Independent body/ information	None/Don't know
				%				
Region (GB)								
North	41	26	21	18	18	14	14	24
Midlands	40	27	14	15	15	15	13	24
South	39	26	17	18	16	17	14	24

Number of respondents 2,034

The Social Group definition is as follows:

A   Professionals such as doctors, surgeons, solicitors, senior business executives and managers, and high ranking grades of the Services.

B   People with very responsible jobs such as university lecturers, heads of local government departments, middle management in business, qualified scientists, bank managers, police inspectors, and upper grades of the Services.

C1 All others doing non-manual jobs; nurses, technicians, pharmacists, salesmen, publicans, people in clerical positions, police sergeants/constables, and middle ranks of the Services.

C2 Skilled manual workers/craftsmen who have served apprenticeships; foremen, manual workers with special qualifications such as long distance lorry drivers, security officers, and lower grades of Services.

D   Semi-skilled and unskilled manual workers, including labourers and mates of occupations in the C2 grade and people serving apprenticeships; machine minders, farm labourers, bus and railway conductors, laboratory assistants, postmen, door-to-door and van salesmen.

E   Those on lowest levels of subsistence including pensioners, casual workers, and others with minimum levels of income.

Source: Adapted from National Consumer Council (1999, Table 6, p. 34)

Table 4.3 Good practice in financial information and advice: Those who made financial decision (Any) and those who did not (None)

How much do you agree or disagree with the following statements?

Financial decision in the past five years	Agree strongly		Agree slightly		Neither/nor		Disagree slightly		Disagree strongly		Don't know	
	Any	None	Any	None	Any	None	Any	None	Any	None	Any	None
	%	%	%	%	%	%	%	%	%	%	%	%
It is difficult to compare similar products provided by different companies	30	22	34	22	14	20	10	4	5	3	8	29
It is difficult to get advice that is truly independent	31	19	30	22	15	22	10	4	6	5	8	29
Advisers usually make it clear if advice is based on companies they are linked	23	14	28	19	15	22	14	8	11	6	10	31

Table 4.3 Good practice in financial information and advice: Those who made financial decision (Any) and those who did not (None) (continued)

How much do you agree or disagree with the following statements?

	Agree strongly		Agree slightly		Neither/nor		Disagree slightly		Disagree strongly		Don't know	
Financial decision in the past five years	*Any*	*None*	*Any*	*None*	*Any*	*None*	*Any*	*None*	*Any*	*None*	*Any*	*None*
	%	%	%	%	%	%	%	%	%	%	%	%
Advisers usually make it clear how much commission they will get	11	11	13	11	13	20	20	11	34	19	10	30
Information provided is usually clear and easy to understand	10	9	24	12	14	22	24	15	21	15	6	27

Survey respondents include those who made any financial decision in the past five years (number surveyed 1,375) and those who made no financial decisions in the past five years (number surveyed 615)

Source: Adapted from National Consumer Council (1999, Table 7, p. 38)

Table 4.4 Good practice in financial advice, 1994 and 1999 compared

	Agree strongly		Agree slightly		Neither/nor		Disagree slightly		Disagree strongly		Don't know	
	1999	1994	1999	1994	1999	1994	1999	1994	1999	1994	1999	1994
It is difficult to get advice on financial services that is, truly independent, that is, to get an adviser who is not linked to any company in particular.	27%	18%	27%	39%	17%	12%	8%	12%	5%	2%	16%	16%
Advisers usually make it clear if their advice on financial products is based around only the company they are linked to.	20%	5%	25%	31%	17%	14%	12%	24%	9%	8%	18%	19%

Table 4.4 Good practice in financial advice, 1994 and 1999 compared (*continued*)

	Agree strongly		Agree slightly		Neither/nor		Disagree slightly		Disagree strongly		Don't know	
	1999	1994	1999	1994	1999	1994	1999	1994	1999	1994	1999	1994
Information provided on financial services is usually clear and easy to understand.	10%	2%	20%	20%	16%	13%	21%	38%	19%	17%	14%	10%

Number of survey respondents – 1999: 2,034   1994: 2,060

Source: Adapted from National Consumer Council (1999, Table 8, p. 38)

Credit Counselling Service (CCCS), independent advice centres and local-authority-provided services. In 2001, for example, 10 major banks provided support of around £2.3 million to external money advice projects. This kind of support is clearly in the banks' own interests as well. Good advice can help a customer assume a realistic, manageable burden of debt; banks' credit collection costs are correspondingly reduced.

The attitudes and respective advice and information provided by UK banks have been subjected to considerable scrutiny and overhauls during recent years. A new version of the Code of Banking Practice (the first such code became effective in 1992) was published in the summer of 1997. This pledged that the banks would do more to help consumers experiencing financial difficulty. A NCC review of how the 1994 code of banking practice was working reported in 1997 and found that: 'Overall, we conclude that the code is not working – local branches, especially, need much more guidance and training if they are to meet its provisions'. The NCC's (1997) subsequent recommendations were designed to help banks meet the new 1997 code of practice.

The NCC proposed *inter alia* more understanding, sympathy and discretion by local bankers in dealing with financial difficulty. The Guidance Notes that accompany the Banking Code were recently re-issued and became effective from 31 March 2002. A copy of the full Guidance Notes can be seen on the BBA's website (at www.bba.org.uk). This new guidance requires (BBA, 2002, p. 26) subscribers to:

- have procedures in place to help customers in financial difficulty;
- provide straightforward information in plain English on how they deal with customers having financial problems;
- develop a budget with the customer which gives them adequate funds for day-to-day expenses;
- consider a full range of options for dealing with the customer's problems; and
- work with the customers' nominated money adviser.

Following these revisions, the BBA published (in February 2002) a leaflet that explains what they (the customers) can expect from their banks if they get into financial difficulties. Other UK initiatives in this area include the National Debtline project (exploring the business case for telephone debt advice and how it can best be offered) run by the Money Advice Trust (MAT) and the 'common financial statement' pilot exercise. The latter is an attempt to standardise the financial statement used by money advisers and their creditors.

Tailoring products and strategies

Universal banking, basic banking services promoting financial literacy and closing the information gap are important responses to financial exclusion. They are also concerned with 'tailoring' or 'matching' products to consumer needs and with developing the appropriate respective strategies. This wider context covers new kinds of financial products and related aspects like affordability, risk assessment and delivery systems.

The FSA (2002, p. 87) suggest that 'affordability' is part of the other issues that are addressed in developing appropriate products that seek to meet the needs of excluded or marginalised customers. This is quite simply because 'appropriate' financial products have to be 'affordable'. The objective here has to be developing and delivering products that are not just cheap, but are also good value for money. This latter point has been strongly emphasised by the Association of British Insurers (FSA, 2000, para 7.4.7).

Kempson and Whyley (1999a, ch. 5) explored (using UK survey evidence) the appropriate product design and delivery needed to help combat financial exclusion. Many of the product requirements of the financially excluded are similar to those of any consumer:

- simplicity and transparency;
- cost and value for money;
- and appropriate marketing.

Whilst others are more specific to households on low income:

- need for greater flexibility;
- and appropriate delivery mechanisms.

They found that most financial products available at the time failed to meet one or more of these criteria. They also suggested that in many cases it was difficult to see how the criteria could be met via relatively minor changes in existing products.

On the banking front, the development of the basic banking account is clearly a major step forward. However, US experience suggests that more research is still needed to deliver, sustain and develop these products to meet the needs of those who are currently un-banked (FSA, 2000, para 7.51). Nevertheless, the growth in numbers of basic bank accounts in the UK augurs well.

Other new product developments in the UK include:

- a project by the Association of British Insurers to design a new savings product to meet the needs identified by non-savers (FSA, 2000, para 7.55);
- the Stakeholder Pension designed to meet the needs of many people who presently lack a pension and want one (FSA, 2002, para 7.56–7.57);
- the development of insurance policies through affinity groups offer the potential of economies of scale that can lower cost (FSA, 2000, para 7.58);
- The Child Trust Fund is expected to be available from 2005. This is aimed at developing savings and assets amongst future generations. It will be a universal account that is opened for all children at birth via an initial government endowment.

(In following sections of this chapter we will explore other new credit products that are being developed via new institutional arrangements).

Risk assessment and the pricing of risk are key product characteristics that bear heavily on financial exclusion. Two respective strategic and economic issues are:

(i)   making more accurate risk assessments; and
(ii) then developing appropriate risk-reducing techniques to handle these risks.

This is a classic 'economics approach' to handling the problem and is: (i) concerned with reducing asymmetric information and (ii) risk mitigation techniques of various kinds.

Credit risk assessment has undoubtedly become a more efficient technique, although experiences with higher credit risks are, by definition, less developed (they are usually refused credit by those who apply the techniques) and/or their default rate is apparently higher with credits extended to date.

In the case of insurance products, the most common proposal for risk mitigation is via risk pooling through affinity groups (FSA, 2000, para 7.37). One example is the 'insured with rent' schemes for home contents insurance. Here, local authorities provide policies at the same rate to all without assessing the individual risk of tenants. Nevertheless, such affinity group solutions do have their limitations. For one thing, they require quite large groups of participants to provide a spread of risk. Another problem is that such a group-based product may not match the needs of all its individual group members.

Widening access to credit is related not only to how risk is assessed, but also to how well it is managed. Some credit suppliers do not use formal credit scoring. Instead, they rely on the acquisition of new customers through personal recommendation. Credit limits are increased in steps as credit experience is gained with these customers; agents visit clients weekly to collect repayments. The downside is that the cost of this kind of credit is high. Credit unions and other such schemes provide other possibilities.

Another aspect of banking strategy that bears on financial exclusion is delivery systems. The closure of UK bank and building society branches has stimulated concern and criticism from many customer groups and lobbies. The banks are looking to technology and partnerships with other organisations to widen access. Many believe that technology alone cannot improve financial inclusion. One problem is that of literacy and familiarity with these more sophisticated delivery vehicles. Another is the need for clearer advice, better information and more face-to-face contact. And these technology-based products do not offer the kind of tight and close control invariably demanded by marginalised consumers.

An interesting and useful initiative in the UK has been that of community select committees: see Collard *et al* (2003). These are set up to consult systematically with intended beneficiaries about the relative merits of the different types of solution being proposed to help combat financial exclusion. They are modelled on the parliamentary department select committees. These committees can also be used to involve stakeholders in policy and service development. Collard *et al* (2003) describe the methodology and some results of these new community select committees.

Other institutional arrangements

Increasing access to financial services involves many other institutional arrangements for product development and delivery. We have already discussed the key role of the Post Office in the new Universal Bank approach. We also saw that the early promise and potential of supermarkets (so called 'thin banking') has not apparently materialised. Where supermarkets move into financial services, they (like the banks) tend to focus on more affluent customers who can be cross-sold a range of products. (FSA, 2000, para 7.8).

Not-for-profit organisations comprise a third group of organisations that are targeted to help reduce financial exclusion. These include credit unions, local exchange trading schemes and various forms of community bank. The present Labour Government has enthusiastically supported the development of the CU (credit union) movement as a means of reducing financial exclusion. CUs are well-established in countries like the United States and Ireland. They are essentially financial co-operatives that are based on the principles of open membership, democratic control, limited interest on capital, equal distribution of any surplus, education and federalisation. The 1999 Treasury Report showed there are 829 credit unions in the UK with assets of £445 million.

Fuller (1998, p. 145) describes CUs as Britain's 'best kept secret'. CUs are essentially 'self help' groups, mutual financial co-operatives that provide convenient and accessible savings and loans products to their members. Although long regarded as the poor relation of the UK financial services industry, the CUs (with total members of around 375,000) came under a new regulatory regime administered by the FSA in the summer of 2002 (on 2 July). Not only did this require the CUs to keep a tighter control on their financial positions, it also allowed them to borrow funds from a wider range of sources. Government sees CUs as an important place for savings, a source of low-cost credit for low income groups and they also provide a first rung on the ladder of financial services for young people (Helen Liddell, Treasury economic secretary quoted in *The Guardian* – Jones [1998]). CUs in this context encourage small savings and can be a stepping-stone to these kinds of financial services (FSA, 2000, para 7.13). The FSA (2000, para 7.20) points out, however, that a major gap in our knowledge is the extent to which CUs are used by people who would otherwise be financially excluded.

HM Treasury PAT 14 (1999) enthusiastically supported the development of the CU movement. They (Melani Johnson, MP) recommended:

> We want to see a new central services organisation (CSO) set up to develop credit unions in Britain. This is a vital link to provide effective impetus to credit union growth, with due emphasis on credit unions serving deprived communities. While details of CSO structure and finance have yet to be worked out, I want to see the current momentum accelerated. I am confident that the credit union movement will respond to the opportunities and work with banks in developing a detailed business plan.

The FSA (2000, paras 7.14 and 7.15) point out, though, that despite the work of a small number of progressive CUs, they have been slow to develop in Britain. Research on CUs in the UK is also comparatively sparse compared with the US. The FSA (2000, para 7.14) survey shows that by the end of the 1990s, CUs covered less than one per cent of the British population (compared with Eire 45 per cent and Canada 16 per cent: see BBA 2000, p. 22) and around 40 per cent of British credit unions are at the fringes of economic viability.

Nevertheless, growth accelerated during the latter part of the 1990s. About 50 new CUs were established annually with an annual increase in membership and assets of about 20 per cent (HM Treasury, 1999b). The movement is particularly strong in Northern Ireland and the North of England.

The FSA survey (2000, paras 7.15–7.16) suggests that CUs need to change considerably if they are to become viable and sustainable over the longer term in providing financial services. CUs need to move towards a 'virtuous circle' of development: they have to attract more savings, leading to bigger loans, which leads to higher income, bigger reserves, more savings, more members and so on (Jones, 1998). Successful credit unions have to be attractive propositions to those who can access mainstream financial services. A successful CU also has to be able to give savers a better return than they get from a bank or building society (ABCUL, 1999, p. 10).

Research on the growth of Scottish CUs draws attention to other important factors: these include the need for a high demand for loans from the outset; a mix of members who can save as well as borrow; and those who run credit unions must emulate good practice in other credit unions. Other key desiderata are strong leadership, professional management, a core group of active volunteers, effective organisation and promotion work, appropriate operational resources, IT infrastructure and good IT skills amongst its staff, ability to offer a range of high quality services and good business sense and strategic planning skills: see FSA, 2000, paras 7.15 and 7.16 and National Credit Union Strategy Working Group (2001).

One in six CUs are work-based, but they comprise around 70 per cent of CU assets. Consequently, there are many community-based CUs and these make up around half of all CU members, but have few assets. Only four out of 257 CUs have any employees (BBA, 2000, p. 22). The BBA (2000, p. 22) points out that most UK branch-based banks support local credit unions; for example, they recognise the role that CUs can play in attracting people to use basic financial services and they provide a viable alternative to loan sharks.

Banks tend to view community-based credit unions as potential partners and not competitors. The BBA (2000, p. 23) lists many examples of banks' involvement with CUs and these include:

- In 1999 Alliance & Leicester began supporting the Sefton Credit Union in Liverpool. It provided office furniture, PCs, all printing needs and helped with a marketing campaign.
- Bank of Scotland provided a free secondee to the Scottish Council of Voluntary Organisation CU to develop and implement a marketing strategy in order to increase membership.
- Barclays provides free banking services to 30 community-based CUs.
- HSBC has developed a training package for start-up CUs.
- Lloyds TSB provides free banking for normal account transactions for community CUs.
- The Co-operative Bank provides a wide range of support, including free banking for CUs.
- RBS, Bank of Scotland and Clydesdale Bank launched a 'Credit Union Health Check' pilot programme to help improve the sustainability of individual CUs.

A key recommendation of the 1999 Credit Union Task Force (set up by the Treasury following PAT 14) was the development of a CSO (Central Services Organisation), which would *inter alia* provide back-office, IT, treasury, training and business planning and financial management for CU members. This CSO would have a primary aim to 'promote credit union growth and development in Britain'.

CUs, then, appear to offer significant potential for development and help in tackling the problems of financial exclusion. However, a lot remains to be done and a great deal of activity and change are currently under way in the UK. Again, CUs illustrate the 'partnership route' (co-operating with the main banks) pursued in the UK and the role of Government as 'mediator and facilitator'. The development of CUs is also a reminder of the wider role and potentials of regional banking and continental-style savings banks with their emphasis on lower income groups and so-called 'social banking'.

There has also been growing interest in the development of community banks: see, for example, The University of Salford (2001). The FSA (2000, para 7.22) suggests there is considerable support for community banks among groups like the unemployed, lone parents and others who presently are at the periphery of banking services. The main banks, however, appear cautious about this concept and are focusing their (presently very limited) support on experimenting with a very small range of models. At the time of the FSA (2000) survey, two such experiments (in Portsmouth and Salford) were being supported. To date, community banking is still pretty embryonic in the UK.

Community Development Financial Institutions (CDFIs) are locally owned and controlled. They look to raise funds from grants, local investments and commercial loans. These funds are used to provide access to moderately-priced loans for people who are financially excluded: see Macfarlane *et al* (2002). CUs in the UK are the most numerous providers of community finances. CDFIs are proposed to complement and support the development of CUs. CDFIs generally cover five categories of organisations: CUs, community development loan funds, micro-finance funds, mutual guarantee societies and social banks. We will explore their business sector roles in a bit more detail in the following section.

CUs, CDFIs and 'not-for-profit' institutions also raise the wider question of mutuality and the role of building societies. Building societies appear to have many attractive features in the fight against financial exclusion. A major positive factor for tackling financial exclusion is the apparent strong belief in the movement of the continued importance of the branch as a sales outlet and the important role of the branch in the wider community. More generally, the question has been raised whether mutuality can fill the gap caused by financial exclusion: see, for example, Rossiter (ed.) (1997). In the UK the whole concept of mutuality has recently been questioned again in the wake of the problems faced by Standard Life, Europe's biggest mutual insurance company.

Nevertheless, the concept of mutuality is being re-explored in the context of combating financial exclusion. The mutual financial services sector comprises the building societies; mutual and co-operative insurance companies; credit unions; and friendly societies. Research indicates that consumers are attracted to mutual organisations when they understand their nature and role (Rossiter (ed.), 2001, p. 82). The 'new mutuals' (see, for example, Conaty in Rossiter [ed.] [1997]) include the credit unions and new initiatives like the Aston Reinvestment Trust (ART)'s SHARE fund for social investment in Birmingham (launched on 27 June 1997). Waite's (2001) recent study also underscores mutual financial services and the 'New Mutualism' of the present Government as an important way forward.

PAT 14 (HM Treasury, 1999a) also emphasised (besides CUs) two other schemes: Insurance with Rent (IWR) and further development of the DSS Social Fund. IWR is where social landlords (local authorities and housing associations) arrange property insurance cover for tenants via group policies. Although the take-up of these schemes has been 'disappointing', they are growing in number and size (FSA, 2000, para 7.27). There is also increasing interest in how they might be extended. PAT 14 also recommended that the DSS Social Fund be developed as a vehicle for those unable to access credit from mainstream providers.

Finally, local exchange trading schemes (LETS) may also be able to help people living on low incomes. For example, it may be able to extend interest free credit facilities via local trading activity (FSA, 2000, para 7.23). Nevertheless, the evidence to date suggests that the impact of LETS on financial exclusion is marginal at best.

SMEs and micro credit (Microfinance)

The importance and role of SMEs and micro businesses in the generation of economic and social welfare are widely accepted. The concept of an enterprising economy and the increasing importance of fostering entrepreneurship reflect the economic importance of the small business sector. A Bank of England (2002) study shows that firms with less than 100 employees account for 99.8 per cent of the total business population, 44.7 per cent of turnover and over 55 per cent of employment.

The UK has been subjected to several major 'inquiries' into the role of banks and small business finance that reach back to the 1930s; the most recent of these is the Cruickshank (2000) review. A common theme that runs through SME studies and discussions is the existence of a 'finance gap': this is usually identified as an equity gap and a lending gap. The Cruickshank (2000) review found (on the equity gap) a supply side 'market failure' for additional equity, especially in the range £100,000 to £500,000. Although there is little evidence of a supply side gap on the lending side, there does appear to be a kind of 'matching' gap. Matching the kind of finance available to that needed is not always easy or even possible.

In this context, the role of bank finance is especially significant. Indeed, there is some evidence of a kind of 'substitution effect' as bank lending is used (often inappropriately) to plug the gaps in the supply of equity finance and/or an inability to obtain the required kind of lending. The supply of finance to SMEs is dominated by the clearing banks. The ESRC Centre for Business Research, Cambridge (2000) showed that bank finance accounted for around 61 per cent of external SME finance in 1997–1999 compared with 48 per cent in 1995–1997.

These gaps in SME finance are well documented; undoubtedly they are important and a major policy challenge; and they comprise a corresponding important part of the overall financial exclusion debate. But it is the micro business end of this spectrum and its location in deprived and other marginalised consumer segments that comprise that subset of financial exclusion of more direct relevance to the present review. Bank of England (2000b) and PAT 3 (HM Treasury, 1999b), for example, are concerned specifically with this segment.

PAT 3 (1999b, p. 2) on Enterprise and Social Exclusion recommended three actions:

- a national strategy conveying commitment and direction from central government;
- strong links with regional and local organisations, and with the private sector, in order to translate that strategy into action; and
- clear responsibility for who does what and for who drives the overall programme forward.

PAT 3 framed its key recommendations against this background:

- The SBS (Small Business Service) should develop a clear strategy to promote enterprise and business growth in deprived areas. This strategy should help to co-ordinate the many organisations involved, have a clear sense of direction and should promote best practice.
- Government should encourage banks to serve poor areas and also provide Government initiatives where the market mechanism is not enough. Two funding windows were recommended on an experimental basis – a national challenge fund for new financing initiatives and a loan guarantee facility to support borrowing from the banks.
- Support for reforms by Government to increase incentives to move from welfare to work, including self-employment.

PAT 3 identified three key factors that might constrain small firms in accessing external finance – asymmetric information, high monitoring costs and higher objective risk. These factors are often accentuated in business located in deprived areas (Bank of England, 2000b, p. 19).

The role of the Community Finance Initiative (CFI) covers a diverse range of initiatives that are targeted to provide alternative sources of funding to business and social enterprises. CDFIs are specialist enterprises that help wider community development via credit provisions and related services to otherwise excluded groups. As we have seen, CDFIs often operate as mutual and non-profit organisations. Since 1998, it is apparent that community development finance has experienced rapid and intensive policy interest and development. Alongside the HM Treasury (PAT) focus, Bank of England review and the mandate of the SBS to promote enterprise (including micro and social enterprise), the following may also be noted:

- The Phoenix Fund under the SBS has £90 million to distribute over three years to support CDFIs and other enterprise development initiatives.
- In 2000 the Social Investment Task Force developed five recommendations to enhance investment in enterprises in under-invested areas.
- Regional and local authorities are developing new strategies to help enterprising firms.

Some banks and building societies have played a critical role in their support of CDFIs.

Nevertheless, CDFI partnerships with banks have not yet achieved the kind of commercial viability found in the US and elsewhere. The UK has not yet seen banks developing specialised subsidiaries akin to community development corporations in the US.

Community development finance is differentiated from so-called 'soft loan funds' in several ways. These latter funds are subsidised funds established by the public sector or through enterprise support agencies (often with help from the banks). There are 200 or so loan and equity funds in the UK that have been established mainly to provide 'last resort lending' to the SME sector. Most of these are soft-loan funds and many have performed badly.

The Bank of England (2000b) surveys in considerable detail all of the major finance sources for small businesses in deprived (financially excluded or marginalised) communities. Although the banks extend a significant volume of lending (on commercial terms) to businesses in deprived areas, businesses that are 'near bankable' or 'marginal' are, by definition, less able to access bank finance. The challenge (to bankers and others) 'lies in nurturing marginal and near-bankable business to reach this (bankable status) stage' (Bank of England, 2000b, p. 21).

Micro credit or microfinance refers to the provision of small loans (usually much less than £5000). This kind of lending can be very risky and costly (for example, the respective administrative costs). Many commercial banks make micro loans (Bank of England, 2000b. p. 25). Most micro-credit programmes (like other business-orientated CFIs) provide significant business support services alongside their lending activities. The largest micro-credit programme in the UK has been the Princes Trust (established in 1976), funded by a combination of public sector performance contracts and private sector funding (from companies, trusts and individuals). Barclays, Lloyds TSB, HSBC and Natwest provided a £6 million syndicated loan, matched by the DfES, in 1997.

The BBA (2002, p. 30) reports on its support for businesses in deprived communities. The UK banking industry is implementing the recommendations of the Social Investment Task Force; these include the support of the Community Investment Tax Credit, Community Development Venture Funds and the setting up of the Community Development Finance Association. Alongside these moves, the banks are further developing their own initiatives; for example, they contributed £3.4 million to CDFIs in 2001. The Social Investment Task Force also recommends that banks publish local level data on their lending activities in deprived areas (to help encourage competitive forces). Data on the first such industry-wide exercise were published by BBA (2002) and these data go beyond the recommendation of the Task Force: Table 4.5 is an extract of the kind of data they now publish and make available on lending to deprived areas. In the year to end June 2001, bank lending to small business in deprived areas grew slower than lending to business across the UK and the average lending margin was higher (at 3.7 per cent compared with 2.8 per cent): see BBA (2002, p. 31).

As we have seen, bank involvement in deprived areas is by no means limited to providing traditional banking facilities. Banks appear to be acknowledging their potential as 'emerging' markets (Bank of England, 2000b, p. 33); there are many indicators of this. For example, NatWest has established a Community Development Banking Unit and Barclays has increased the size of its social banking team. The banks participate in several initiatives to promote financial inclusion. The banks are active supporters of different CFIs. Natwest was a founder of the Women's Employment Enterprise and Training Unit (WEETU)/Full Circle Fund (Norfolk) and the Aston Reinvestment Trust (Birmingham). The banks also support several loan schemes.

Table 4.5 Disclosure of bank activity in deprived areas to the British Bankers Association: lending to small business aggregate data

Post Code	Current Accounts (Number)	Loans <£10k (Volume £000s)	Loans >£10k (Volume £000s)	Overdrafts <£10k (Volume £000s)	Overdrafts >£10k (Volume £000s)	Deposits (Volume £000s)	Start-ups (Number)
			Lending to Small Businesses Aggregate Data				
B1 1	224	-£100	-£2,041	-£59	-£512	£2,618	69
B1 2	244	-£29	-£1,284	-£75	-£606	£18,022	42
B1 3	330	-£130	-£2,811	-£150	-£1,079	£2,746	55
B2 4	278	*	-£404	-£121	-£987	£1,976	51
B2 5	248	-£27	-£1,384	-£61	-£936	£3,466	51
B3 1	457	-£84	-£5,982	-£161	-£1,199	£5,100	100
B3 2	458	*	-£1,954	-£87	-£1,122	£9,808	53
B3 3	353	-£22	-£2,816	-£69	-£2,271	£5,366	53
B4 6	374	-£61	-£1,000	-£139	-£4,925	£4,139	37
B4 7	228	-£27	-£719	-£80	-£702	£2,411	60

Source: Adapted from BBA (2002, Appendix)

Finally, we may note the Bank of England[1] stated on 29 April 2004:

> In recent years there has been a major expansion in government resources devoted to small firms. The Small Business Service was set up in 2000 as an executive agency of the DTI, to be a centre of excellence on the whole range of small business issues, including access to finance. The Bank has strongly supported the SBS, including seconding one of its senior staff to be the SBS' first Director of Investment and SME Finance from 2000 to 2003.

and added:

> Given the substantial improvement in information flows over the past ten years and the growing importance of the SBS in addressing access to finance issues in the government's Action Plan for Small Business, there is no longer a need for the Bank to be involved in these issues. The principal objective of supporting an improvement in the financing relationship has been achieved, and stepping back from the work stream will avoid potential overlap and duplication with the work of the SBS... Active contact with small firms will continue through the work of the Bank's regional agents. And the Bank will continue to take a keen interest in the financial health of the whole corporate sector.

It is clear that the Bank regards the SBS as a key plank of its initiatives in the small business sector.

Regulation and financial exclusion

Regulation, in all its forms, has an important bearing on financial exclusion. As we have seen, the regulatory 'model' of deregulation (the liberalising of banking structure and conduct rules), together with other key drivers like competition (intensified via deregulation), globalisation (which also intensifies competition and facilitates the shareholder value model) and technology (changing the underlying economics of banking), are all important factors that bear in varying ways on financial exclusion. Generally, they appear to intensify financial exclusion for marginalised societal groups. In this section, we focus on the particular features of the UK banking and financial system

---

[1] http://www.bankofengland.co.uk/pressreleases/2004/051.htm

regulatory apparatus that are currently under debate or reform in the context of financial exclusion.

It is clear that the UK regulatory authorities are attuned and focused on the problems of financial exclusion. Both the Bank of England and the FSA, for example, are expending considerable efforts in studying, monitoring and tackling financial exclusion in a variety of ways. An essential feature of the UK approach is partnership between the private sector (the banks) and a wide variety of other organisations.

One regulatory issue has been the problems of opening a new bank account without an extensive set of identity documents (FSA, 2002, para 7.69); the Cruickshank report was critical of the UK money laundering regulations (BBA, 2000, p. 11). The 'know your customer' (KYC) rules have been developed to combat money laundering. Discussions between the Treasury and the banking industry have led the way to more balance in these rules (FSA, 2002, para 7.70). The Joint Money Laundering Steering Group's (JMLSG) new Guidance Notes gives the industry some discretion in how it can best meet anti-money laundering priorities (Mullen, 2002). These Guidance Notes were produced by and for six financial services trade associations (that span banking, insurance and investment management), although in practice the greatest emphasis is likely to remain on banking since that is the route of most money laundering. The JMLSG, working with the BBA, will need to ensure that 'KYC' checks do not contribute to financial exclusion.

The FSA (2002, para 7.70) refers to a need for 'simpler', more appropriate' regulations for some of the new savings, pensions and other investment products. The challenge is to protect the low-income consumer, but not to price them out of the market. In the wake of a series of 'mis-selling' scandals, regulation has been increased. However, it is argued that this new and comparatively strict regulation falls more heavily on those products with a comparatively low premium or contribution rate. The FSA suggests that simple benchmarked products should require a much lighter regulation in the future since the potential for mis-selling should be reduced significantly.

We saw earlier that one key sector in tackling financial exclusion is the new, embryonic not-for-profit organisations. These encompass credit unions, the proposed community banks and CDFIs in general. To some extent, these CDFIs have developed in an environment of regulatory 'benign neglect'; this has helped CDFIs to launch and to innovate. However, it has also created regulatory uncertainty. Since most CDFIs are still comparatively small-scale operations, their underlying need is for relatively 'permissive' or 'facilitating' regulation. The latter needs to allow for an established model or choice of models, for carrying out their business with the needed flexibility. At the same time, though, consumer protection and lessening the chances of 'systemic risk events' in this sector have to be recognised. The FSA (2000, para 7.72) points out that the community bank initiatives in Portsmouth and Salford were delayed because of the need to comply with the complexities of the FSA's rules. In this context, the UK Government has recently lifted some of the restrictions in the Credit Union Act 1979 so as to facilitate credit union growth. Schemes (like share protection) are also being explored to help maintain depositor confidence.

So far, stronger affirmative action (like the US Community Reinvestment Act [CRA]) has not been adopted. Donovan and Palmer (1999, p. 55), for example, point that there is no empirical evidence for 'redlining' in UK credit markets (of individuals being discriminated against on the basis of their geographic location); they also point out a number of practical difficulties of implementing this kind of regulation (which is itself contentious in the US). Donovan and Palmer (1999, p. 55) favour instead a kind of 'Community Reinvestment Disclosure Act' which would 'name and shame' banks and building societies into more positive work on financial exclusion and in lower income areas. We saw that the BBA (2002) has begun to publish aggregate data on lending to lower income customer groups.

The present UK view is to see what if any kind of legislation might be needed once some more experience has been gained with the present and evolving voluntary moves by the financial services industry (FSA, 2000, para 7.74). The FSA (2000, paras 7.75–7.77) point out that there have been calls to strengthen the voluntary codes of practice issued by trade associations that together comprise an important part of the overall financial services regulatory apparatus. In the area of pension coverage, several UK studies suggest that compulsion is not the best way forward from a consumer perspective.

Recently in the UK there has been growing concern about the sub-prime credit market. The impact of financial exclusion is attenuated in this market segment. Compared with one credit card in circulation thirty years ago, for example, there are now around 1,300 different types of card in the UK. This modern credit society exacerbates the disadvantages experienced by the financially excluded. Without access to mainstream credit, the financially excluded have to use expensive sub-prime lenders. In June 2004 the National Consumer Council submitted a 'super-complaint' on the sub-prime credit market (specifically, home credit or 'doorstep lending') to the Office of Fair Trading (see Hutton, 2004).

Many positive regulatory developments (both by government and by the financial services industry itself) have already taken place and several more are being studied and/or planned. In this developing environment, it is important that financial exclusion is monitored efficiently in order to see if it is being reduced and to see if other, further approaches are needed. The FSA (2000, paras 7.79–7.86) survey the different indicators of social and financial exclusion that have been proposed and which are now beginning to be monitored more systematically in the UK. Many of these are aggregate, industry-wide data. As we saw earlier, there are also growing calls for more voluntary disclosure by the banks on what they are doing. The New Economics Foundation (FSA, 2000, para 7.83) has outlined the essential features of this kind of disclosure. In this monitoring process, there are calls to be vigilant about new forms of exclusion and whether financial exclusion is being superseded by 'marginalisation', where new products and delivery systems either fail to meet consumer needs or do not integrate them into mainstream financial services.

Conclusions

Three things at least are clear from this chapter. First, in the UK financial exclusion and increasing access to financial services have several facets; there are several kinds of financial exclusion and sometimes these can be interrelated. Financial exclusion is correspondingly a complex problem and no single policy approach can tackle all aspects.

Second, the UK banking industry during the past two decades has been going through one of its most fundamental periods of change ever experienced. We saw earlier that technology, deregulation, globalisation and intensifying competition are key strategic drivers. Technology is facilitating the development of new kinds of delivery channels, products and services. Technological developments facilitate the development of new kinds of banks with novel value propositions. A fundamental problem is that increasing competition and the drive towards shareholder value maximisation can produce an increasing bank strategic focus on profitable, 'value-adding' customers. As a result, the promotion of competition (via deregulation and other moves) and increasing financial inclusion may be argued to be mutually exclusive. If this apparent dichotomy is the result of asymmetric information then an appropriate response is to close this information gap so that presently marginal and excluded customer segments can be priced and managed more effectively. If this is not the main cause of financial exclusion, then some kind of policy action is needed. *Ceteris paribus* the preferred action is that which does not distort the competitive process.

A third point to be noted is that tackling financial exclusion is a top priority of the present UK Government. A range of initiatives are being developed. Unlike in the US, the UK policy response to date has been characterised by Government as 'facilitator and mediator', with an emphasis on a partnership approach. In this 'model', the banks, other financial institutions and the post office have a key role to play in helping to overcome financial exclusion.

5
Financial Exclusion in the US

Introduction

The US banking and financial services industry is one of the most advanced in the world. In many respects, the US is a kind of 'pacemaker' in financial services development for other countries. Like the UK, financial exclusion is a major issue in the US; strong Government affirmative action has been one noteworthy response in the US. In all countries experiencing and reacting to financial exclusion, the banks are seen as an indispensable and integral part of the response mechanism. At the same time, one has to be aware of the institutional context of different countries in explaining financial exclusion, its economic consequences and the appropriate policy responses.

The present chapter focuses on the US and what is clear is that the rise of deregulation in financial services sectors, intensifying competition and the rise of the 'value maximisation' model have exposed a growing need to tackle financial exclusion. US experiences (as probably the most strongly market-orientated banking system in the world) correspond closely to those of the UK, although the approach has been more legislation based. There are also important institutional differences between the US and UK (for example, the respective roles of the post office, credit unions and Government affirmative action).

Nature and extent of the problem

In the US, the most detailed and generally respected survey of household finances is the Survey of Consumer Finances (SCF), which is sponsored by the Board of Governors of the Federal Reserve System from which indicators of financial inclusion can be obtained. (The Survey is published every three years – at the time of writing 2001 data were available).

Access to basic banking transactions accounts is an important indicator of whether households use banking services. Chequing and savings accounts (referred to generally as 'transactions accounts' or deposit accounts) are provided to the public by the commercial banks, savings and loans banks and credit unions. Unlike in many European countries, there is no post office savings system in the US. Table 5.1 shows details relating to the financial assets of US households. It can be seen that the proportion of US households that do not have a chequing account that in 2001 was around nine per cent of all families (compared with 9.5 per cent in 1998 – not shown in the Table). Throughout the 1990s there has been a decline in the percentage of families without a transaction account of any kind.

In the 1995, 1998 and 2001 surveys, the socio-economic groups most likely not to have a transaction account were the same:

- those in low income;
- families headed by a person younger than 35 years or older than 75 years;
- to be a non-white or Hispanic respondent;
- and to be in the bottom 25 per cent of the wealth distribution.

Families that do not have deposit accounts are very unlikely to own any other financial asset.

Like the UK, consumers are routinely scored for credit in the US. The three main types of mainstream consumer credit comprise: home-secured loans; installment loans; and revolving credit card loans. With the increased sophistication of credit scoring techniques and respective databases, there has been an increase in the number of mainstream lenders willing to extend credit to sub-prime applications and even to the most risky sub-categories of sub-prime. A higher interest rate is naturally charged to cover the higher potential default risk and the higher monitoring costs.

Despite this trend, low-income households are markedly less likely to have home-secured loans and 'somewhat less likely' to have installment loans. Nevertheless, these crude descriptive data have many limitations. For example, they do not indicate the number of denials of particular societal groups. In the home mortgage market where more detailed data of this kind are collected, however, denial rates appear higher for low income and minority households. These same US home

Table 5.1 Family holdings of financial assets, by selected characteristics of families and type of asset 2001 survey

2001 Survey of Consumer Finance

Family characteristic	Transaction accounts	Certificates of deposit	Savings bonds	Bonds	Stocks	Mutual funds	Retirement accounts	Life insurance	Other managed assets	other	Any financial asset
				Percentage of families holding asset							
All families	90.9	15.7	16.7	3.0	21.3	17.7	52.2	28.0	6.7	9.6	93.1
Percentiles of income											
Less than 20	71.1	10.0	3.9	*	3.9	3.6	13.3	13.9	2.2	6.5	74.9
20–39.9	89.5	14.9	11.4	*	11.8	9.4	33.3	24.2	3.6	10.3	92.9
40–59.9	96.0	17.4	14.2	1.3	16.2	15.8	53.4	26.3	5.5	10.2	98.3
60–79.9	98.7	16.3	24.2	3.7	25.4	20.3	74.4	35.0	8.4	9.2	99.6
80–89.9	99.7	17.5	29.6	3.9	37.9	29.6	84.9	39.1	10.3	11.3	99.8
90–100	99.2	22.1	29.8	12.9	60.7	48.8	88.3	41.9	16.7	12.8	99.7
Age of head (years)											
Less than 35	86.0	6.3	12.7	*	17.4	11.5	45.1	15.0	2.1	10.6	89.2
35–44	90.7	9.8	22.6	2.1	21.6	17.5	61.4	27.0	3.1	9.7	93.3
45–54	92.2	15.2	21.1	2.9	22.1	20.3	63.4	31.1	6.4	9.1	94.4
55–64	93.6	14.4	14.3	6.1	26.6	21.3	59.1	35.8	13.0	11.0	94.8
65–74	93.8	29.7	11.3	3.9	20.5	19.9	44.0	36.7	11.9	8.4	94.6
75 or more	93.7	36.5	12.5	5.8	21.8	19.5	25.7	33.3	11.2	8.2	95.1
Race or ethnicity of respondent											
White non-Hispanic	94.9	18.5	19.5	3.8	24.5	20.9	56.9	29.8	8.2	9.6	96.5
Non-white or Hispanic	78.2	6.7	7.8	0.4	11.0	7.2	37.3	22.3	1.8	9.7	82.4

Table 5.1 Family holdings of financial assets, by selected characteristics of families and type of asset 2001 survey (continued)

2001 Survey of Consumer Finance

Family characteristic	Transaction accounts	Certificates of deposit	Savings bonds	Bonds	Stocks	Mutual funds	Retirement accounts	Life insurance	Other managed assets	other	Any financial asset
				Percentage of families holding asset							
Current work status of head											
Working for someone else	92.4	11.3	19.4	2.0	20.9	17.3	61.5	27.4	5.3	9.7	94.7
Self-employed	95.2	18.8	16.6	6.1	29.8	23.0	58.9	34.7	6.9	12.8	97.4
Retired	88.9	27.1	11.4	4.5	19.6	17.3	29.2	29.0	10.5	8.2	90.8
Other not working	70.3	7.8	7.5	*	13.3	10.9	26.8	12.9	5.6	7.6	72.8
Housing status											
Owner	96.5	20.0	21.2	4.1	27.1	22.7	62.7	34.5	8.9	9.2	97.7
Renter or other	79.3	6.7	7.2	0.7	9.3	7.1	30.4	14.3	2.0	10.5	83.5
Percentiles of net worth											
Less than 25	72.4	1.8	4.3	*	5.0	2.5	18.8	6.9	*	8.0	77.3
25–49.9	93.6	8.9	12.8	*	9.5	7.2	45.4	26.1	1.3	8.9	96.5
50–74.9	98.2	23.1	23.5	*	20.3	17.6	63.1	34.5	6.2	9.0	98.9
75–89.9	99.6	30.1	26.0	5.3	41.2	35.8	77.6	41.8	13.8	9.9	99.8
90–100	99.6	27.0	26.3	18.6	64.3	54.8	87.4	48.4	26.6	16.9	100.0

Source: Adapted from the Federal Reserve Bulletin (2003) 'Recent Changes in US Family Finances: Evidence from the 1998 and 2001 Survey of Consumer Finances', January 2003, pp. 1–32, Table 5

mortgage data confirm that sub-prime loans were more concentrated in low-income groups and those with a high percentage of black or Hispanic families.

Dymski and Li (2002), analyse the spatial characteristics of US financial exclusion in some detail and draw attention to the key role of strategic shifts in US commercial banking. They explore the impact of deregulation, globalisation, intensifying competition and the growing dominance of a few megabanks (the product of a strong post-deregulation merger wave) in practically every significant US banking market (Dymski and Li, 2002, p. 5).

Bank mergers and acquisitions are seen as central to the dynamic of the 'standardised customer' who is increasingly targeted by banks. Bank profit-making in this world focuses on maximising the number of customers who will take up the product in question without defaulting. This 'megabanking world' of modern US banking is associated with high bank fixed costs (linked to more expensive product development, product architecture, testing and marketing) and a low marginal cost of servicing customers. Customers for one product, for example, can be targeted (cross-sold) with other products. An expensive, 'old-style' extensive branch network is no longer the sole or most important delivery system for financial products to these kinds of customer segments. The main emphasis is to focus on wealthier households and the better capitalised firms, customers who can produce easier 'value-added' for the banks. These customer relationships have to be nurtured carefully over time and developed through the life cycle of the customers. As one such customer segment is 'fully developed', other new and similar segments have to be sought.

The concept of the 'standardised customer' is not all bad news in the context of financial exclusion. Dymski and Li (2002) focused on the more profitable standardised customer segments. At the other end of the lending spectrum, standardised sub-prime lending pools have been securitised (via asset-backed securities issues) in the US. This is a 'good result' since it allows the asset-backed securities (ABS) market to develop as another vehicle to economise on bank capital and help tackle the problems of financial exclusion. Since the US domestic ABS market is the biggest and most developed market of its kind in the world, this kind of development is of obvious interest to other countries.

In the US, practically all adults receive social security payments on reaching the age of retirement. These payments are related to contributions made over an individual's working life. Around half of all families also have individual or employment-based pensions as well. In these latter pensions, defined contribution schemes comprise around 80 per cent of the total. Again, low-income households and those with non-white and Hispanic members are less likely to have retirement (defined-contribution) schemes. Insurance coverage reveals a similar picture. The 1998 and 2001 SCF data show that these same groups are less likely to own a cash-value life insurance policy (in the US these double as life insurance and as a savings vehicle).

Causes and consequences

Again the similarities to UK experiences are marked. US research shows that those groups without monthly savings do not have deposit accounts because they believe they do not need them; 'don't write enough cheques', 'do not like dealing with bank' and 'not having enough money' appear to be the major reasons cited for not having a transactions account. Other common reasons cited are the cost of bank fees, minimum balance requirements, privacy and the formality of dealing with a bank. See Table 5.2 for reasons cited as to why use households do not have transactions accounts. Interestingly, US survey data do not support the hypothesis that the closing of bank branches is a significant factor in explaining why people do not have a bank account.

Poor or non-existent credit histories are the main reasons why people are excluded from prime lending by mainstream lenders in the US. As a result, this borrowing segment is usually confined to sub-prime or sub-sub-prime markets. FSA (2000, para 6.24) reports on the empirical evidence of poor loan payment history by this segment: they produce data showing that a significantly high percentage of low-income US households have bad credit records that credit score them outside of the range of prime loans by conventional credit scoring models. Other studies point to lack of awareness by some low income families that they could qualify for lower-cost prime loans. There is also some evidence that racial and other ethnic minority discrimination can play at least a secondary role in explaining exclusion from prime credit in the US.

There appears to be a paucity of available US research since 1995 on why a disproportionate proportion of low-income households and households headed by a minority group figure do not have pension accounts in order to supplement social security. However, the FSA (2000) survey of the US system suggests several possible explanations. For example, social security replaces almost 60 per cent of the income of a typical low-wage worker; consequently, s/he has much less need to

Table 5.2   Distribution of reasons cited by respondents for their families' not having a chequing account, by reason, 1989, 1992, 1995, 1998, and 2001 surveys

Reason	1989	1992	1995 Per cent	1998	2001
Do not write enough cheques to make it worthwhile	34.4	30.6	25.3	28.4	28.6
Minimum balance is too high	7.7	8.7	8.8	8.6	6.5
Do not like dealing with banks	15.0	15.2	18.6	18.5	22.6
Service charges are too high	8.6	11.2	8.4	11.0	10.2
Cannot manage or balance a chequing account	5.0	6.7	8.0	7.2	6.6
No bank has convenient hours or location	1.3	0.8	1.2	1.2	0.4
Do not have enough money	21.2	21.1	20.0	12.9	14.0
Credit problems	**	0.7	1.4	2.7	3.6
Do not need/want an account	**	3.2	4.9	6.3	5.1
Other	6.8	1.8	3.4	3.2	2.4
Total	100.0	100.0	100.0	100.0	100.0

** For the 1989 SCF, these responses were not available and are most likely part of the other category.
Source: Adapted from the Federal Reserve Bulletin (2003) 'Recent Changes in US Family Finances: Evidence from the 1998 and 2001 Survey of Consumer Finances', January 2003, pp. 1–32, Box Example

acquire extra income. Other reasons include the fact that a disproportionate proportion of low-income workers work for small firms that do not provide pension benefits.

The consequences of financial exclusion are generally similar to UK experiences. As a result, the following will focus primarily on the special or unique features of US experiences that are worthy of note.

As in the UK, the main consequence of being without a deposit account is the need to make other arrangements to meet payment needs, like cashing cheques and making 'long-distance' payments (FSA, 2000, para 6.33). Although the available data do not appear robust, it appears that around 50 per cent at least of 'un-banked' households are able to cash their paycheques at banks or credit unions that do not charge fees. These banks often have business relationships with those who employ the un-banked customers. There are also community banks that cash Government transfer cheques as a kind of 'community service'. Other encashment avenues include grocery stores, who (as in the UK) often require that such customers spend a proportion of the cash in store. Long-distance payments, on the other hand, are handled mainly by money orders (easily available at post office branches and many kinds of commercial operations).

In the case of exclusion from mainstream credit, practically all households can access alternative sources. However, these alternatives are typically costly, inconvenient and provide very limited protection to the consumer. In states where usury ceilings do not apply, borrowers not eligible for prime and sub-prime loans may borrow at much higher rates (APRs of 200 per cent or more) from small-loan finance companies and payday lenders. These latter lenders developed in the late-1980s and they have grown 'explosively' during the past decade; APRs on these loans often exceed 500 per cent.

Those unable to get unsecured consumer loans have three basic alternatives: rent-to-own shops (equivalent to lease-purchase outlets in the UK); car-title lenders; and pawn shops. However, these alternatives are costly to individuals excluded from bank credit; APRs of 150–200 per cent for these kinds of borrowing are common.

Exclusion from pensions and savings-orientated life insurance has the same kinds of consequences as in the UK and other countries. In the US, practically all adults are covered by social security. There is a corresponding, but less generous Government support programme (Supplementary Security Income, or SSI) for those older, lower-income adults that are not within the scope of social security. None of these social security payments provide adults with an easy living and they need to be supplemented to provide a comfortable retirement.

Responses to financial exclusion in the US

During the past 30 years, a wide range of policies have either been implemented or proposed in the US. Tackling exclusion from bank deposit accounts, for example, was one of the aims of the famous (and still hotly debated) Community Reinvestment Act (CRA). This legislation was originally instituted in 1977 and has been modified subsequently a number of times. The basic aim of the CRA (1977 and 1989) is to help ensure that financial institutions meet the credit needs of their respective communities. Under this legislation, federal bank regulatory agencies subject banks to a 'service' test; banks are rated on their lending and other services record.

This CRA rating (banks are graded 'outstanding', 'satisfactory', 'needs to improve' and 'substantial non-compliance') really bites when a bank wishes to open (but not to close) a branch or to merge with a competitor. In order to address such applications, regulators are obliged to evaluate a bank's CRA record (Donovan and Palmer, 1999, p. 54). The CRA requires data that relate to the economic and geographic profile of their customers; a major impetus to the CRA was the US bank practice of 'redlining'.[1] Overall CRA ratings are the result of several evaluation tests. Lending, service and investment are weighted (BBA, 2002, pp. 38 & 39):

- Lending (50%) – mortgages, consumer finance and small firms
- Service (25%) – distribution of branches; record of opening and closing; other delivery channels; and range of services and products
- Investments (25%) – type and amount of investment mode by community.

This assessment is based on a bank's record of helping to meet the credit needs of its entire neighbourhood, consistent with prudent, sound and safe banking operations. The CRA examination is conducted every two years.

The CRA and related legislation (like the Home Mortgage Disclosure Act and the Fair Housing Act) have attracted a great deal of policy and academic interest: see, for example, Donovan and Palmer (1999), Office of Fair Trading (1999), FSA (2000) and BBA (2002). US banks point to the CRA stimulating billions of dollars of lending for home purchase or to small business (BBA, 2002, p. 3a). Although CRA does not require unprofitable lending, much of this kind of lending has been at rates of return that are usually lower than mainstream interest rates. In the US,

---

[1] These were implicit or explicit red lines on map showing where a bank would not lend because of the racial or economic characteristics of the community.

as we have seen, a good CRA record is considered by regulators in evaluating applications for new branches, branch location and mergers and acquisitions. A compliant bank is also helped by direct Government loans (or risk guarantees) to customers in deprived areas, together with tax breaks.

CRA is strong affirmative action. Despite its apparent and alleged benefits, there are no reliable data on its impact on bank branch closings (FSA 2000, para 6.42). It does appear, however, to have had a significant impact on lending in low-income neighbourhoods. Nevertheless, CRA is a policy response to a particular institutional feature of US banking, the practice of redlining. The use of banking procedures that segregated customers on racial and geographic lines was still used in US banking as recently on the mid-1970s (BBA, 2002, p. 37). The UK and the EU countries surveyed in this report have not apparently inherited this kind of historic legacy (Donovan & Palmer, 1999, p. 55). Although the CRA-type approach is not favoured in countries like the UK (see, for example, Donovan & Palmer [1999, p. 55] and [BBA 2002, p. 40]), a 'Community Investment Disclosure' kind of approach does seem to have wider support.

Other important areas of legislation in the US that bear on the problems of financial exclusion are rules ('fair lending' acts) and anti-discrimination laws (see Rose, 2000, pp. 615–619). The former rules mandate that the customer is given full details about the cost and essential requirements of a loan, lease agreement or other financial service. Anti-discrimination laws prevent categorising loan customers by age, sex, rate, national origin and other specific features. Prominent legislation in these two areas includes the Truth-in-Lending Act 1968 and the Equal Credit Opportunity Act 1974 (as well as the CRA, of course). Recent regulatory concern in the US has been about predatory lending, especially home-secured loans. An important regulatory response has been the 1994 Home Ownership and Equity Protection Act.

Another important policy response in the US has been the 'basic' or 'lifeline' bank accounts. Under these proposals (enacted into law by a few states), banks are required to offer a low-cost chequing account with a low minimum balance requirement. These kinds of lifeline banking laws were first proposed in several states in the early to mid-1980s. By the late 1990s, seven states had enacted the legislation for lifeline banking accounts (Doyle *et al* 1998). Generally, though, the evidence suggests that the effect to date of these kinds of accounts in reducing financial exclusion within the US is apparently small: see, for example, Doyle *et al* (1998, p. 5) and FSA (2000, para 6.44). Doyle *et al* (1998, p. 5) propose in this context that … 'measures that increase the convenience of banking services and inform customers of the potential savings from using these services could prove effective in assisting the un-banked'.

A third public policy measure has focused on reducing the cost of turning to alternatives. The respective legislation sets ceilings on the fees chargeable by cheque-cashing outlets (FSA, 2000, para 6.45). However, in several cases they are not binding since the ceilings have been set higher than the corresponding free market rates.

During the second half of the 1990s, the federal government and many states reduced their costs of administering welfare and benefits programmes through a greater use of electronic payments. Hogarth and O'Donnell (1999, p. 460) point out that these initiatives are likely to have their biggest impact among lower-income families, the demographic group with the lowest rate of bank account ownership and those least familiar with electronic transactions.

Legislation was enacted in the US that required all federal transfer payments to be made electronically by 1999 (FSA, 2000, para 6.46). As part of this initiative, the US Treasury urged banks to create 'electronic transfer accounts' (ETAs). These ETAs have to accept electronic transfers from the federal Governments; they carry no minimum balance requirement; they allow the account owner to withdraw funds using an ATM card; and banks are only allowed to charge the account holder a $3 per month maintenance fee. The FSA (2000, para 6.46) survey report on 'grounds for scepticism' for believing that these ETAs will bring many unbanked into the system. For example, they question whether the highly restricted nature of an ETA merits the title of bank account.

Other US public policy initiatives aimed at expanding deposit ownership include enhancing the Earned Income Tax Credit; the objective being to raise the income of low-income households. Other proposals include expanding educational efforts to teach the benefits of saving and budgeting. On the lending front, regulators have been directed at the loan policies (like interest rates and fees charged) of lenders in the alternative financial sectors. In many cases, however, as the alternative financial sectors have become bigger and more politically sophisticated, they have lobbied successfully to have such usury laws reduced.

In the area of pensions, savings-oriented life insurance and other savings products, several US innovations are noteworthy. In an important and influential book. Sherraden (1991) argued that tax incentives to encourage savings do not benefit lower-income groups since these pay little tax. He proposed that the Governments create 'Individual Development Accounts (IDAs)'. The basic idea is to encourage low-income households to save by Government offering to match their savings for approved purposes (like retirement).

During the past decade, many not-for-profit community development groups have created small-scale IDA programmes. Several state Governments have also started their own IDAs. In his 2000 State of the Union address, President Clinton (building on the IDA concept) proposed that the federal Governments create 'Retirement Savings Accounts' for low-income households.

A note on select bank trends and developments

The preceding section noted the importance of 'institutional context' in understanding the contemporary setting of particular kinds of financial exclusion and the respective policy response. A good example is the historic US banking practice of 'redlining' and the CRA response. We also noted earlier the Dymski and Li (2002) study on the spatial characteristics of US financial exclusion. In particular, the growing dominance of the 'megabank' and the central dynamic within the respective consolidation process of value maximisation and the 'standardised customer'. In this section, we draw attention to some selected, related developments.

Table 5.3 shows trends in US bank asset concentration, 1984 versus 2000. For present purposes, several developments are germane. The asset share of the smallest banks (under $1 billion) has been reduced from 36.6 per cent in 1984 to 16.1 per cent in 2000. These community banks specialise generally in retail or consumer banking; this group of banks is clearly decreasing in both number and relative importance. On the other hand, bigger banks (including regional or super-regional banks) are increasing in importance.

Similar trends are also apparent amongst US savings institutions: these are savings associations and savings banks. US savings associations have historically focused on residential mortgages whilst the savings (S & L's) banks are more diversified, covering residential mortgages and holding commercial loans, corporate bonds and corporate stock. Table 5.4 shows a similar trend to that of US banking generally, a strong movement towards larger size and greater concentration. Traditionally, US savings banks have also been organised as mutuals. Following the banking and property problems of the 1980s

Table 5.3 US bank asset concentration, 1984 versus 2002

	2000				1984			
	Number	Percentage of total	Assets	Percentage of total	Number	Percentage of total	Assets	Percentage of total
All FDIC-insured Commercial Banks	8,315		$6,238.7		14,483		$2,508.9	
1. Under $100 million	4,842	58.2	231.2	3.7	12,044	83.2	404.2	16.1
2. $100 million–$1 billion	3,087	37.0	773.0	12.4	2,161	14.9	513.9	20.5
3. $1–$10 billion	313	3.8	884.1	14.2	254	1.7	725.9	28.9
4. $10 billion or more	82	1.0	4,350.4	69.7	24	0.2	864.8	34.5

Source: Saunders and Cornett (2002, Table 2.3)

Table 5.4 US savings institution asset concentration, 1992 versus 2000 (in billions of dollars)

	2000				1992			
	Number	Percentage of total	Assets	Percentage of total	Number	Percentage of total	Assets	Percentage of total
All FDIC-insured Savings Institutions	1,590		$1,222.6		2,391		$1,035.2	
1. Under $100 million	624	39.3	30.9	2.5	1,109	46.4	55,946	5.4
2. $100 million–$1 billion	819	51.5	245.5	20.1	1,093	45.7	315,246	30.5
3. $1–$10 billion	107	6.7	207.8	17.0	181	7.6	479,526	46.3
4. $10 billion or more	40	2.5	738.4	60.4	8	0.3	184,476	17.8

Source: Saunders and Cornett (2002, Table 2.13)

and early 1990s, respectively, many savings banks (like other savings institutions) gave up their mutual organisations in favour of stock charters.

With total assets of $441.6 billion at end-2000, credit unions comprise a substantial sub-sector of US savings institutions. Credit unions (CUs) are non-profit depository institutions that are mutually organised and run by their members.

CUs are forbidden from serving the general public. Members are required to have a common bond of occupation and the main objective of a CU is to meet the depository and lending needs of their members. The members own the CU, which also has tax exempt status (since it is a non-profit organisation). There were just over 10,000 credit unions in 2000, making them the most numerous of US depository institutions.

As CUs have grown in number and size, they have expanded their services. Many US bankers complain that CUs unfairly compete with small commercial banks (the community banks) that have historically been the main lenders in small towns. Bankers complain that their tax exempt status gives them a subsidy borne by taxpayers (Saunders and Cornett, 2002, p. 51). The CUs response is that this tax-exempt status benefits its members and, therefore, enhances the social good.

Two lawsuits were filed in 1997 by the banking industry in its drive to restrict the widening membership rules governing CUs (following a 1982 legal ruling). The Supreme Court sided (1998) with the banks. In April 1998, however, the US House of Representatives overwhelmingly endorsed a bill (signed into law in August 1998) that not only allowed CUs to retain their existing members ... 'but allowed CUs to accept new groups of members – including small businesses and low-income communities – that were not considered part of the 'common bond' of membership by the Supreme Court ruling' (Saunders and Cornett, 2002, p. 51).

Having fought off these challenges and expanded their powers, the CUs have been able to expand even further into the traditional territory of the banks. Credit union membership has almost doubled since 1982. In 2001, they had 82.6 million members and $500 billion in assets (Arnfield, 2002). The Credit Union Membership Access Act 1998 gives CUs ... 'the specified mission of meeting the credit and savings needs of consumers, especially persons of modest means' (Arnfield, 2002, p. 67). Table 5.5 provides some select CU and bank comparisons in 2001.

Table 5.5 Credit union and bank comparisons, 2001

	CUs	*Banks*
Net income as percentage average total assets	0.95	1.16
Equity as percentage total assets	10.93	9.09
Loan delinquency ratio (%)	0.85	1.41
Average size ($ million)	50	813
Total assets ($ billion)	515	6,569

Source: Adapted from Arnfield (2002, p. 31)

Conclusions: Bank strategic implications

Although US experiences bear many similarities to those of the UK, there are some marked differences in policy approaches by Governments and their respective relationships with banks. These differences reflect the different institutional structures of the two countries and their respective 'political' approach, itself a component of the corresponding institutional structure and its development trajectory. These country and system differences must be borne in mind in comparing and evaluating policy responses and bank strategies.

In all country studies, there are apparently no easy solutions or 'quick fixes' to financial exclusion.

The US 'model' for dealing with financial exclusion is quite eclectic, but affirmative action (via CRA) is a strong feature. Basic or 'lifeline' bank accounts and IDA-type facilities are also noteworthy US initiatives. Basic banking accounts lie naturally at the heart of many countries' efforts to increase financial inclusion. They are a common feature in the US although we do not appear to have adequate data to evaluate their success, although the limited data suggest that they can make significant inroads. In the US, the role of credit unions and the wider savings institutions sectors are also noteworthy.

6
Financial Exclusion in Europe

Introduction

The European banking and financial services sector has also been subject recently to intense deregulation and globalisation pressures within the process of completing the internal market and the development of European monetary union. Within the EU, financial exclusion has emerged as a major issue. Like UK and US experiences, the apparent dichotomy between the 'free competition' model and the 'public good' aspects of basic financial services has emerged as a major policy and bank strategic challenge. In all countries experiencing and reacting to financial exclusion, the banks are seen as an indispensable and integral part of the response mechanism. As noted before, one always has to be aware of the institutional context of different countries in explaining financial exclusion, its economic consequences and the appropriate policy responses.

This chapter explores recent experiences in continental European countries. As EU policymakers are beginning to pay more attention to financial exclusion, bankers and the financial services industry are being reminded of their central role in this debate. The apparent 'threat' of affirmative regulatory action by the EU has to be tempered by the possible strategic 'opportunities' that the emerging financial exclusion agenda might raise for European banks.

At the same time, continental European banks have traditionally had a stronger focus on retail banking via the development of many kinds of specialised banks. The concepts of 'regional banking' and 'social banking' are also comparatively well-developed in Europe. Nevertheless, as deregulation and globalisation continue to emphasise 'value added' and the shareholder model, the experiences of the UK and US became more interesting to the emerging EU landscape. One thing that is apparent is that the institutional structure of different countries' banking and financial sectors has an important bearing on the nature of financial exclusion and how it is (and can be best) tackled. That is not to say that one country's experiences may not be relevant and helpful to another. An unqualified adoption of another country's 'model' for handling financial exclusion, however, may not be appropriate without considering the respective institutional contexts.

Policy and strategic context

Many of the same policy issues and bank strategic challenges concerning financial exclusion are emerging in EU banking systems. Like the UK and US, deregulation, intensifying competition, technological developments and high rates of innovation are strong drivers in EU financial sectors.

Nevertheless, there is a wide variety of different historic and institutional settings in EU banking systems in which these modern economic forces have been unleashed. As a result, there are still markedly different levels of financial sector development and varying policies for tackling issues like financial exclusion. Social and financial exclusion, however, are now high on the EU policy agenda.

Tackling financial (and other kinds of) exclusion is being increasingly recognised as a major issue in the EU. Pollin & Riva (2002, p. 213) point out in this connection:

> Financial exclusion is one face of this problem and access to financial services is increasingly becoming an important step in the path towards inclusion into the labour market and into social life in general. Furthermore, financial inclusion can contribute to substantial cost savings for the community. It also encourages consumers to take ethical values into account to a greater extent when making their choices. Finally, it can bring new activities and customers to the financial system.

Increasing EU interest and banking awareness of these issues confirm that (like the UK and US) financial exclusion will be of increasing policy and bank strategic concern. Banks will increasingly be exhorted (and perhaps mandated) to make their contribution towards greater financial inclusion. Many banks may see these developments as a strategic opportunity to re-affirm their own missions (especially in regional and 'social banking') and competitive positioning.

As in the US and UK, financial exclusion lies at the heart of a modern and challenging political-economic-social dilemma. Free market economies with an emphasis on deregulation, liberalisation and globalisation emphasise the 'driver' of bank and consumer free choice. As we have seen earlier, though, this same value maximisation model appears to foster more banking consolidation and a growing emphasis on the 'standardised customer'. Customers in this economy are targeted and developed in terms of their Life-Time-Value (LTV). This process appears to help marginalise increasingly some groups in society from even basic financial services. These developments seem to conflict 'head on' with the fundamental right of every citizen to be able to access basic services.

At its most basic level, this fundamental dichotomy comes down to 'competition' versus the 'public good' element of basic banking and financial services (see Revell 1989 and 1991). At the same time, this apparent dichotomy is being attenuated by other, often wider developments; these include the increasing withdrawal of the state from social security provision. An increasingly aging population together with technology and other developments, are reducing the proportion of labour in active, long-term employment and this has put inexorable pressures on 'old style' European pension arrangements. The need to save and the requirement to develop private sector provision to meet the growing 'pensions time-bomb' all revolve to varying degrees around financial (and wider social) exclusion. There is also a growing awareness of the need to help 'fire up' regional and peripheral economies. Governments across Europe are recognising the longer term economic and social importance of developing regional economies and fostering entrepreneurship at all levels, starting with individuals and micro businesses. Access to basic banking and financial services is increasingly recognised as the essential 'lubricant' and 'facilitator' of these desired economic and social developments.

Pollin & Riva (2002, p. 215) point out that exclusion appears to be a growing problem in the EU. Around 18 per cent of the EU population (some 65 million people) live on less than 60 per cent of the median national income (this is the low-income threshold set to measure relative poverty). Only social transfers within the EU have prevented a larger proportion of the EU population moving into these poverty zones.

The EC have affirmed via the European Social Agenda the concept of a social policy that embraces increased inclusion as a major, 'ongoing target'. Improved forms of governance that bring together the EU, member states, local and regional authorities, non-Governments organisations and enterprises of all kinds are seen as the way forward. Within the framework of market liberalisation, the 'general economic interest missions' are the means by which a balance may be struck between competition and protecting more vulnerable consumers. Nevertheless, the position of the EU remains imprecise, undeveloped and not altogether transparent on these general interest missions in the context of financial exclusion and areas related to it (like the provision of basic banking services and the development of regional financial infrastructure).

The inception of the process of completing the EU internal market (began in the mid-1980s) released and has continued to intensify competitive forces that have attenuated the free market model and the kind of dichotomy discussed earlier. Up until then, many basic banking services were effectively cross-subsidised by more profitable ('super-profitable') activities. Increasing competition, a greater emphasis on efficiency and value-added, and the rise of techniques like RAROC pricing all operated to eliminate the old cross-subsidy models of banking. Concomitant trends like securitisation (and banks competing with open financial markets) and globalisation (increasing competition further, offering banks enhanced opportunities to exploit economies of scale and scope, but also subjecting them to a widening ownership base and more rigorous external tests of their market-based efficiency) conspired to eliminate the economic acceptability of these kinds of historic cross-subsidies. As a result, banks were no longer able to offer some basic banking services practically free.

The development of Euroland is a further globalising and deregulating event in this same context. At an EU banking level, there still remains scope for considerable consolidation compared to the US: for example, the five largest EU banks still account for around 12 per cent of the market compared with 22 per cent from the US. Technology further facilitates the process of customer segmentation, more focussed delivery, targeted services support and the overall selection, monitoring and strategic development of profitable market segments. These are exactly the same kinds of trends and developments that we discussed earlier in our survey of UK and US experiences. For many EU countries, the problems of financial exclusion and the respective strategic and policy responses are likely to be even more dramatic and far reaching than US and UK experiences. This is because many EU countries began their EU-induced trajectory of deregulation and globalisation from a more highly regulated (i.e. more protected) and less financially developed position. This rapid 'catching up' is likely to exacerbate the problems and challenges associated with financial exclusion in all of it forms.

The 5th International Conference of Financial Services was held in Gothenburg (Sweden) in 2000 (EC, 2001). This conference expressed considerable concern at the increasing exclusion from financial services of those with limited means. The conference explored many means to help overcome financial exclusion, but emphasised that all such action is highly dependent on the availability of reliable data on the extent of discrimination and the respective impact of different measures. They called on all parties (financial services providers, national Governments and the EC) to collate, publicise and monitor such data.

Select comparative data

This section focuses on some select comparative data on financial exclusion in the EU. Table 6.1 is adapted from the Eurobarometer survey and reproduced by Pollin & Riva (2002, Table 5.1). It draws attention to several aspects of contemporary European access to a basic bank account:

- Although most countries have considerable financial inclusion for this basic product, there are some noteworthy exceptions.
- Countries with an apparently high level (10 per cent or more of population excluded) of financial exclusion for these basic banking facilities include:
  - Greece (17.9% +)
  - Ireland (16.7% +)
  - Italy (22.4% +)
  - Austria (13.5% +)
  - Portugal (16.7% +)
  - UK (10.6% +)
- There is considerable variation among the countries surveyed. Financial inclusion varies from 99.1 per cent (Denmark) to 70.4 per cent (Italy).

One has to exercise care in interpreting these data. These apparent differences, for example, are also related to the means of payment most commonly used. Payments systems in European countries differ in

Table 6.1   Availability of a personal current account, giro account or similar (%)

Country	Yes	No	No response	Country	Yes	No	No response
Belgium	92.7	5.1	2.0	Luxembourg	94.1	3.9	1.7
Denmark	99.1	0.7	0.2	Netherlands	98.9	0.5	0.6
Germany	96.5	2.9	0.6	Austria	81.4	13.5	5.1
Greece	78.9	17.9	3.2	Portugal	81.6	16.7	1.8
Spain	91.6	6.9	1.5	Finland	96.7	1.5	1.7
France	96.3	2.8	1.0	Sweden	98.0	1.6	0.4
Ireland	79.6	16.7	3.7	UK	87.7	10.6	1.6
Italy	70.4	22.4	7.2	EU 15	89.1	8.6	2.2

Source: Adapted from Eurobarometer survey 52, Financial Services, Europeans and Financial Services (May 2000) and Ruozi and Anderloni (eds) (2000, Table 5.1)

many important respects, including supply structure, user preferences and control mechanisms.

Table 6.2 summarises some comparative data on the different use of payment services in the main European countries. Cash in circula-

Table 6.2   Payment services in the main European countries

(a) Cash in circulation/GDP ratio in the main European industrialised countries

	Belgium	France	Germany	Italy	The Netherlands	United Kingdom	Spain
1981	10.1	5.4	5.5	6.4	6.6	4.2	n.a
1991	6.0	4.3	6.5	5.4	6.9	2.7	n.a
1999	5.1	3.3	6.6	6.0	4.6	2.9	9.7*

* This figure refers to 1998

(b) Per capita transactions settled with instruments other than cash

	Belgium	France	Germany	Italy	The Netherlands	United Kingdom	Spain
1998	122.5	181.1	166.5	42.5	154.5	150.8	46.2

(c) Cash deposits by the public as a percentage of GDP

	Belgium	France	Germany	Italy	The Netherlands	United Kingdom
1991	13.6	19.9	15.6	31	17	45.8
1999	20.1	21.7	21.2	33.3	30.4	59.8

Source: Adapted from Leonelli (2002, pp. 176–178)

tion/GDP varied (in 1999) from 2.9 per cent (UK) to 9.7 per cent (Spain). Per capita transactions settled with instruments other than cash (in 1998) similarly varied markedly: from 42.5 per cent (Italy) and 46.2 per cent (Spain) to 166.5 per cent (Germany). Similarly, cash deposits by the public as a percentage of GDP varied (in 1999) from 20.1 per cent (Belgium) to 59.8 per cent (UK).

Various European countries like Spain and Italy, are still characterised by a comparatively high use of cash (see Carbó, Humphrey and López del Paso, 2003), which may be an indicator of a 'hidden economy'. It may also reflect (and help to perpetuate) some kind of financial exclusion. This phenomenon *inter alia* is worthy of further explanation, especially in the context of the rapidly growing electronic payments instruments and related facilities throughout Europe.

European countries also differ markedly in their use of the post office and postgiro account (Leonelli, 2002, pp. 184–185). For example the post office appears to be important in all of the countries listed in Table 6.2, although of lesser comparative importance in Belgium and the Netherlands.

On the demand side, the Eurobarometer survey (Pollin & Riva, 2002) report on very much the same kind of socio-economic characteristics of those excluded as similar surveys in the UK and US. These kinds of characteristics include a high proportion of those who are less well off, women, older and younger members of society, the less educated and the unemployed.

The Eurobarometer survey found that around 52 per cent of those excluded had never had a bank account. Once again, though, Europe is characterised by considerable heterogeneity. Table 6.3 shows figures for the number of people who have never had bank current accounts they range from 13 per cent (Denmark) to 63 per cent in Finland; Sweden (at 22%) lies at the bottom end of this range whereas Italy (55%) is towards the higher end. Age (the young and older age groups), low income groups and psychological barriers are apparent factors why those excluded have never had a bank account.

Another interesting statistic revealed by the Eurobarometer survey is that on average 21 per cent of those excluded voluntarily closed their accounts. Again there was a marked heterogeneity between countries, ranging from a high of 50 per cent (Netherlands) who closed their accounts voluntarily to a low of 2.8 per cent (France).

The exclusion of low-income groups is the result of many factors: these include the lack of suitable services associated with the account, lack of appropriate products, geographic access and pricing. Refusal by

Table 6.3   People in European countries who have never had a current account (%)

Country	Yes	No	NSP	Country	Yes	No	NSP
Belgium	40.7	50.9	8.4	Luxembourg	40.0	48.3	11.7
Denmark	13.0	52.0	35.0	Netherlands	17.1	82.9	0.0
Germany	55.4	33.3	11.3	Austria	32.6	58.8	8.6
Greece	46.9	49.6	3.5	Portugal	54.9	38.0	7.2
Spain	48.4	45.4	6.2	Finland	63.1	6.7	30.3
France	59.8	25.8	14.4	Sweden	22.9	68.7	8.4
Ireland	61.1	34.8	4.2	UK	45.8	50.6	3.6
Italy	55.7	41.8	2.5	EU 15	51.6	43.3	5.0

Source: Adapted from the Eurobarometer survey 52, Financial Services, Europeans and Financial Services (May 2000) and Ruozi and Anderloni (eds) (2002, Table 5.2)

the banks to open a current account is not a major barrier at the European level. Similarly, banks closing accounts is apparently not the most important factor explaining such closures.

One important driver of European banking strategy has been that of cost reduction:[1] a process consistent with deregulation, intensifying competition and value maximisation. This has *inter alia* prompted banks to incentivise their customers (via lower costs) to use new distribution technologies (ATMs, home banking etc). The banks have correspondingly embarked on rationalisation programmes to cut distribution costs. As a result, branches have been cut back and many of these cuts have fallen heavily on rural and poor urban areas, the least profitable geographical locales.

We saw earlier that UK bank branches reduced markedly between 1989 and 1999 by around 30 per cent (a drop in the number of branches from 17,000 to 12,000). These same trends are apparent in Scandinavia. In Germany, over 8,000 branches closed as a result of bank mergers and rationalisations: total branches declined from 66,663 (1996) to 58,546 (1999); these reductions applied over all banking sectors in Germany, including the savings banks and co-operative banks (Reifner *et al*, 2000, p. 23). In France, on the other hand, bank branches increased over 1996 to 1999. French banks were unable to compete in the deposit

---

[1]   Maximising productive efficiency (lowering cost/income ratios) is a necessary condition for shareholder value maximisation. Necessary and sufficient conditions require that banks' internal capital allocation (risk/return) efficiency is also maximised.

market in terms of price and this prompted them to differentiate themselves via proximity and service quality. (See Revell 1987 for a detailed discussion on bank mergers and the role of large banks).

Responding to financial exclusion in Europe

The 'Gothenburg Declaration' of the 5th International Conference on Financial Services considered the following measures indispensable in Europe:

- The enforceable right to a bank account that gives access to the most advanced and sophisticated means of the modern payments system.
- Minimum standards for financial services that guarantee quality, encompassing usury ceilings, risk coverage and exploitation of vulnerable groups.
- A bankruptcy procedure that gives all individuals an effective and structured new start in society.

Other needed strategies identified at Gothenburg include:

- accessible pension schemes that provide lifetime coverage;
- micro-lending for job creation and self-employment;
- accessible consumer credit with usury limits and default protection;
- affordable mortgage loans;
- and insurance cover for the most significant social risks.

The Gothenburg Declaration concluded with a plan for greater co-operation by all parties to address the growing challenges of financial exclusion.

Pollin & Riva (2002) identify the following 'models' for tackling financial exclusion within Europe: the Market, the Voluntary Role of Banks, the Government as Mediator and the Government as Legislator. These are briefly discussed below.

The market: Spain, Greece, Ireland and Italy

These countries are characterised *inter alia* by a comparatively low use of banking services and the lack of banking system products designed specifically for vulnerable groups. In these countries the markets are not currently equipped to solve the problem of financial exclusion. The problems of financial exclusion are not addressed in a direct way.

In all of these countries, financial exclusion will have to move much higher up the political agenda. Ireland and Italy have already began to develop some initiatives and there is considerable academic and policy research already well-developed in Italy: see, for example, Pollin & Riva (2002) and Anderloni (2003).

Spain is somewhat of an exception in this grouping in that 'private market' approaches are comparatively developed. Although it is true that financial exclusion has not been high on the political agenda in Spain compared with other countries, various institutions (like the savings bank foundations) pursue objectives aimed at helping to reduce financial exclusion. During the past five years the Spanish savings banks and their Confederation have publicly stated their high interest in reducing financial exclusion. Spanish savings banks offer banking products that are designed specifically for vulnerable groups. In this context, Spain is probably among the leading countries in tackling financial exclusion via 'private market' means.

The voluntary role of banks: France, Germany and Belgium

In France, Germany and Belgium, public opinion and Government attention have stimulated professional associations to develop Charters to deal with the problem of financial exclusion. Germany, followed by Belgium and France, has taken this route; Finland and the Netherlands have also adopted this approach. The Central Credit Committee (2KA) of the German professional association launched their Charter in June 1995 with the slogan 'Current accounts for all' (Girokonto für Jedermann'). Nevertheless, doubts have been expressed as to whether the German growth in 'current accounts for all' is really bringing in the financially excluded (Pollin & Riva, 2002, p. 228).

The Belgian Government launched the debate on financial exclusion in 1996 and in July 1997 the Belgium Banking Association launched a Charter that specified the right of every individual living in Belgium to open a savings account irrespective of the amount and frequency of income. Account holders have to agree to deposit their salaries in this account, which encompasses three basic transactions: manual or electronic monetary payment (transactions are blocked that result in an overdraft), receiving deposits (cash, cheques etc) and withdrawals (a bank card is also possible). Opening these accounts must not be connected with the sale of other financial products and a minimum service level is also specified. The Ombudsman monitors application of the Charter and also acts as mediator between customers and banks.

In France a similar kind of Charter encompassing basic banking services was drawn up in 1992. The several basic banking services include the possibility of an ATM card, long-distance payment and a system of cheques whose number can be restricted with the agreement of the customer. Nevertheless, various groups in France have questioned whether the banks merely pay lip service to this Charter: for example, around 7 per cent of new account requests have apparently been rejected.

The government as mediator: the UK and the attempt in France

As we noted in Chapter 4, the UK Government has set up 18 PATs (Policy Action Teams) to address social exclusion; PAT 14 deals with financial exclusion; PAT 14 and the Cruickshank (2000) review encompass the Government's framework of action. The need to reform social security and Government pressure on the banking sector via threats to mandate a universal banking service conspired to convince the banking sector to set up the kind of basic banking services advocated in PAT 14. The UK Government promotion of co-operation between the public and private sectors in tackling financial exclusion; fostering the development of credit unions; increasing financial education and financial literacy of vulnerable groups; annual reporting and banking efforts to reduce financial exclusion by the BBA; and availing of the extensive branch network of the Post Office characterise the UK model of mediation by Governments and public/private sector co-operation.

The French Government has played a strong mediating role by getting consumer protection groups and banking system representatives around a table. Particular attention was focused on basic banking services and the right to open an account. A basic problem and central issue has been that of an undifferentiated (by service level and customer segment) 'universal service'. Bankers argue that this concept is at variance with the principles of safe and sound banking.

The government as legislator: France, Portugal and Sweden

The French Government enacted an anti-exclusion law in July 1998. This law gives any person residing in France the right to open a deposit account. In the absence of a consensus with the banks, Government legislated (17 January, 2001) on the following components of the required basic banking services (Pollin & Riva, 2002, p. 234):

- the opening, maintenance and closure of an account;
- one change of address each year;
- provision (on request) of banking or postal sort codes;
- establishment of a place of payment for bank or post office transfer orders;
- dispatch on a monthly basis of a statement of transactions conducted on the account;
- performance of cash transactions;
- collection of cheques and bank or post office transfer orders;
- deposits and withdrawals of cash at the branch of the body where the account is established;
- payments by standing order, interbank payment order or bank or post office transfer order;
- means of remote consultation of the account balance;
- a card of systematically authorised payments (if the credit institution is able to provide this) on a withdrawal card that allows weekly withdrawals from the credit institution's cash dispensers;
- and two bank cheques per month or equivalent means of payment offering the same services.

This legislation provoked some controversy. Although the procedure of the right to open an account is quite limited, recourse to it is on the increase.

The Portuguese Government also decreed the institution of basic banking services on 10 March 2000. Although bank compliance is voluntary, around 90 per cent of banks were participating by 2001. Under this ruling, basic banking services are required to be available to all, regardless of income or whether they receive social benefit. Banks have some (limited) discretion on fees. The basic services under this legislation include: the opening and management of a current account; a debit card that allows for cash withdrawals from ATMs and making payments; cash transactions at branches; and a biannual statement of account.

Although Swedish banks were required by their Banking Business Act to open accounts, this was not observed in practice. As a result, the Swedish Financial Supervisory Board disseminated a circular (following an earlier one in 1996) in 2000 which emphasised that individuals were still complaining about problems in opening an account. Banks were reminded that this obligation must be upheld. Nevertheless, the banks are only required to open an account; they do not have to provide a means of payment. Although the practice is condemned by the authorities, Swedish banks have the right to refuse payments services and even the issue of cash cards.

Conclusions: Bank strategic implications

Although US and wider European experiences bear many similarities to those of the UK, there are some marked differences in policy approaches by Governments and their respective relationships with banks. These differences reflect the different institutional structures of countries and their respective 'political' approach, itself a component of the corresponding institutional structure and its development trajectory. These country and system differences must be borne in mind in comparing and evaluating policy responses and bank strategies.

In all country studies, there are apparently no easy solutions or 'quick fixes' to financial exclusion. At the same time, in all of the countries surveyed financial exclusion is an increasing problem and one that has moved to the top of many Governments' policy agendas. Market and wider political-economic-social forces have conspired to enhance this policy concern. Within the EU, the EC are increasing their concern and attention with all of the issues associated with exclusion.

As noted in the previous chapters, basic banking accounts lie naturally at the heart of many countries' efforts to increase financial inclusion. They are a common feature of the US and the European countries that we have studied. It is clear that social and financial exclusion moves in the EU will exert continuing, inexorable pressure on the banks to respond. Experiences in countries like France and Sweden have exposed the problems of reconciling universal, non-discriminatory banking (a social objective) with the requirements of safe and sound banking (an economic objective).

It is also clear that there are different 'models' for responding to financial exclusion in Europe. But in all of these, the banks are required to play a key role. Regional and social banking, together with the role of more social-orientated players like the savings banks, are likely to develop a renewed vision in this developing scenario. These banks and others will have to consider whether a proactive and long-term strategy towards helping to reduce financial exclusion is now the way forward.

In many countries, the increasing move by Governments towards using electronic methods to make benefits payments have helped to attenuate the need to tackle financial exclusion. French experiences (like those of the UK) have also indicated the potential important role of the Post Office in tackling financial exclusion. In the following chapter we shall seek to draw together these kinds of findings and consider the overall strategic implications of financial exclusion for the banking industry.

7
European Policy on Financial Exclusion and Bank Strategies

Introduction

This chapter explores three areas. First, we examine the broad European policy response to expanding financial exclusion on Chapter 6 and also discuss the implications for banks. Second, we discuss the kinds of strategies that banks have and might develop in this evolving scenario. Finally, we focus on how economic theory may be able to help explain why financial exclusion occurs and in doing so as to provide some practical insight into how the banking system ('bank strategies') might be developed to combat exclusion.

Market context and European policy responses

Financial exclusion is now a major issue in the EU and in several national member states. It is also evident that financial exclusion appears to be exacerbated by the forces and 'strategic mindset' of financial services firms that are incentivised and facilitated via deregulation. Whilst the economic benefits of liberalisation and greater competition continue to be sought, the free market unaided does not appear capable of solving the financial exclusion problem.

Other kinds of regulatory interference can exacerbate the problem. A good example is money laundering rules (initiated by Basle), which have had the unintended side-effect of making it more difficult for financially excluded groups to access basic financial services. The apparent inexorable withdrawal of the state from social security provision (like pensions) also exacerbates the problem and makes a private sector 'solution' more pressing. At the same time, Governments converting welfare payments into electronic format have accelerated some moves to widen financial inclusion.

All of this adds up to a rather complicated scenario. What seems to be evident is that the private sector solutions alone cannot (will not) solve this problem. Deregulation and other market trends have increased the imperative for financial sector firms to target shareholder value, risk-based pricing, economic capital and overall greater efficiency, both productive (cost/income) and capital allocation (risk and return) efficiencies. Paradoxically in the present context, the new Basel 2 rules for capital adequacy regulation will intensify these trends.

These free market desiderata can produce many desirable 'economic goods'. A higher output of financial services, products tailored more closely to demand, higher rates of innovation, greater bank efficiency, lower prices and improved service quality, to name but a few of the targeted benefits. The overall 'economic good' at a macro level is that the economy is enabled to operate at higher investment levels and on investment schedules that carry higher risk (but better managed and hedged via a more efficient financial services sector). This is the economic model that is actively pursued in Europe via liberalisation, deregulation and globalisation of financial services sectors. Within this process many dimensions of financial inclusion have widened.

Nevertheless, the 'value model' pursued by financial sector firms increasingly emphasises the 'standard customer', the more profitable customer segments. Marginal customers may become ever more excluded. For example, as financial services firms 'desert' particular geographical localities and customer segments, information for assessing respective risks is reduced; asymmetric information problems worsen. Concomitantly, the 'risk pools' for such marginalised groups may also reduce for individual financial services firms; risk becomes less predictable and less amenable to risk pooling.

This is the contemporary and developing scenario that governments face. In one important respect, US experiences (and to a lesser extent, UK) are especially germane to Europe. The US system is in many respects the 'pacemaker', the 'innovation engine', of the development of financial services. On the one hand, financial services are produced more efficiently than in many other countries and are particularly responsive to the 'shareholder model', the free market. On the other hand, this kind of model by itself appears to have the most negative impact on social and financial exclusion.

The same appears true in the UK. Both the US and UK financial sectors are probably the most deregulated and market-orientated in the world. In both countries, significant policy responses also characterise government action. Both the US and UK have seen strong Government action directed at tackling financial exclusion. Strong affirmative action in the US (via CRA) has not been replicated in the UK, but the UK Government has undoubtedly pursued a coercive and directing role.

Historical and institutional setting

It is important to relate financial exclusion to the historic and contemporary institutional setting of a financial system. In the US, for example, 'redlining' led to apparent discrimination and resultant financial exclusion of some societal groups; this apparently required strong affirmative response. In the UK, on the other hand, this kind of redlining has not been a feature of the financial services industry. The UK system also has a history of government 'coercing' and using 'moral suasion' to get its way. The result is an emphasis on Government mediation, self-regulation (the financial services industry and its associations generally responding to the Government's wishes) and public/private and private/private arrangements for tackling financial exclusion. These may not always work in the way intended and may need to be complemented with stronger rules and guidelines, but they reflect the UK model. Like the US, the UK has developed one of the most successful financial sectors in the world. Flexibility, responding to market pressures and a respect for government aims are hallmarks of the British regulatory philosophy.

In many European countries, the historic and institutional apparatus have emphasised more strongly 'public models' and social responsibility. The financial sector systems and strategic mindsets of many European bankers and politicians reflect these ideologies. They are not contrary in any way to UK and US aspirations, but they have impacted on the development of European banking and regulatory thinking in different ways. In Europe, these kinds of models are embodied in political philosophies that are reflected in constitutional constraints like 'solidarite' (France), 'mutuality' (Italy) and the 'social state' (Germany).

These philosophies are reflected at many levels in the way that European banking has evolved. The role of publicly chartered banks, savings banks, regional and social banking all reflect this 'European philosophy'. The 'debate' between 'shareholder value' and 'stockholder value' are other transparent aspects of the continental European approach. In this connection, Schuster (2000, p. 7) points out that in the diffusion of a shareholder value orientation (reporting on a 1997 Coopers and Lybrand survey):

- 90 per cent of enterprises 'pretend' to be focused on the interests of shareholders, but only 34 per cent of them use shareholder value techniques in planning, decision-making and communication.
- Shareholder value plays a rather unimportant role in France, Belgium, Italy, Austria and Spain.
- 'Countries in transition' that are increasingly adopting the entrepreneurial philosophy are Canada, Switzerland, Sweden, the Netherlands and Hungary.
- Shareholder value is increasingly important in the US and UK.

Nevertheless, European banking has been 'on the move' throughout the 1990s and the banking industry's strategic mindset has undoubtedly changed during this period: see Economic Research Europe Ltd (1997) and Gardener *et al* (2002). Hörter (in Schuster [2002, p. 13]) points out in this context: 'Managers – especially those in continental Europe – who neglect shareholders' financial interests have to be aware that their behaviour will no longer be tolerated. Capital is increasingly in the hands of powerful professional fund managers'. The Hörter study is quite clear that shareholder value will increasingly drive European financial services firms: see also Gardener *et al* (2002, 2003). Nevertheless, this survey and discussion illustrate two things. First, continental European banking structures and philosophies have evolved from and still reflect a more public sector and social banking orientation. Second, there is still considerable heterogeneity amongst continental European banking systems.

In a macro, regulatory and political philosophy context, the older European public models are also having to change. We saw in the previous chapter that the EC globalisation, deregulation and liberalisation agenda are reflective of this new approach. At the same time, the European welfare state is at a crossroads and change is already under way. The basic aspirations of these traditional welfare systems remain generally sound. However, their public, non-competitive format does not appear to be consistent with the process of globalisation.

Policy responses to financial exclusion

In this developing market context, we have seen that financial exclusion inevitably becomes an increasing socio-economic and regulatory issue. It is also clear that both at an EU and national state level, financial exclusion is an increasingly important area. Without public and private sector responses, the problem will get worse; this is a basic message of UK and US experiences to date. In the last two chapters, we identified and characterised several 'models' of responses to financial exclusion that have evolved in the UK and these are developed a little and summarised again below:

- *Government Affirmative Action* (US).
- *The Market, but increasing Government and Private Sector Interest* (Spain, Greece, Ireland and Italy).
- *The Voluntary Role of Banks* (France, Germany and Belgium).
- *Government as Mediator* (UK and French attempt).
- *Government as Legislator* (France, Portugal and Sweden).

These 'models' are by no means mutually exclusive ones. In practice, a combination of approaches is often deployed. Where private sector response is not apparent and/or is not working, however, the likelihood and need for a stronger Government-led initiative seems apparent. By the end of the current decade (2010) it seems inconceivable that combating financial exclusion will not be a major priority of all EU-member states.

Governments and regulators will need to address particular attention towards ways of overcoming financial exclusion without disrupting the free market competitive model and disadvantaging some kinds of players. One such 'model' might be targeting a particular objective associated with reducing financial exclusion; assessing the appropriate level of state subsidy (if any) on the basis of agreed social objectives; and then inviting a tender process to select the most efficient private sector firm(s) to implement this societal 'franchise'. So far, this kind of 'model' has been discussed, but not yet explored and developed in practical detail to help tackle financial exclusion.

One relevant finding from both US and UK experiences is the apparent attractiveness of requiring banks to account transparently for their services to excluded and more vulnerable groups in society. The UK approach (via the BBA) where the banks are now disclosing their lending volume to lower income and other 'excluded' groups is a significant step forward.

This kind of disclosure 'fits in' with the free market model – providing such data allows 'the market' to feed this into its overall evaluation of a bank. There is also a marked shortage of these kinds of data.

Bankers, regulators and the public at large need a better understanding of how these data may be related to basic strategies (on the supply side) and the development of marginalised sub-sectors of customers and geographic localities (on the demand side).

Bank strategies and products

'Doing nothing' does not appear to be a viable strategy for any responsible bank. 'Waiting to be told' by Government, public opinion and/or via some other route also appears to be inappropriate. In an age of growing environmental and social awareness, banks need to take a proactive stance. For many kinds of bank (ethical savings banks, credit unions, co-operative banks etc), this is not a difficult strategic mindset. In these sectors of banking, re-affirming such social and longer-term objectives is the way forward. What is also clear from this survey, however, is that the private sector alone cannot tackle the problem.

Nevertheless, 'social responsibility' and key areas like 'regional development' have long been part of the competitive positioning of savings banks, mutuals and many other kinds of banking organisation. In the new world, however, all of these kinds of banks also have to compete increasingly with shareholder-driven banks. In the US and UK, mutuality has come under pressure. Consolidation, 'financial supermarkets' and ever bigger size continue to dominate strategic thinking. We have seen that in this kind of environment, tackling financial exclusion has to be developed strategically as a kind of 'value proposition'. We have seen earlier (in Chapter 3), for example, that when depositors, borrowers and other shareholders understand the meaning and purposes of concepts like 'mutuality', they are willing to support such models. These are strategic challenges that have to be met. Our survey suggests that 'partnership routes' appear to be the best way forward for many initiatives.

Whatever the strategic route chosen by an individual bank or group of like-minded banks (or Government exhorting the banks), the basic issues are:

- matching products to needs;
- pricing, supporting and delivering such products successfully;
- not compromising bank management principles of safety and soundness (which means covering all risks in the bottomline);
- communicating relevant information and helping to improve the financial literacy and finance handling skills of marginal (excluded) customers;

- being responsive to customer needs over their life-cycle;
- often being prepared to take a longer view and exploring new, viable LTV (Life-time Value) concepts.

These desiderata add up to a challenging agenda at best. Some of these (e.g. enhancing financial literacy) may only be tackled effectively in a co-operative, partnership way. UK research has emphasised the need to involve the beneficiaries in the process of product development. In this context, Collard *et al* (2003) examine several new UK products developed to help increase financial inclusion.

The most fundamental problem of all, of course, is developing the appropriate products to match the needs of the financially excluded. Having access to a financial product may not be the answer to financial exclusion; if the product is inappropriate, it may even exacerbate the problem of financial exclusion. An inappropriate product may increase the financial fragility of a customer. For example, excessive pricing and allowing more than a prudent volume of borrowing can lead to an eventual default and an even worse credit rating. At the same time, the psychological distrust of banks and this kind of banking is intensified, attenuating any 'self-exclusion' tendency.

New products and access to them have to be combined with 'suitability for purpose'; this is not an easy proposition to address. In countries like Sweden and France, bankers have objected (often via their own policies) to regulator-induced provision of basic banking services. In order to solve such problems, a more 'co-operative model' is needed. Such a model may also require in some instances state mediation at the very least and strong state direction at the other extreme. This is an area where the savings banks and other organisations who operate supra-bank 'umbrella organisations' might be a good way forward. Why are such 'collective models' needed?

The short answer is economies of scale and scope. Collecting, compiling, monitoring and using risk data on these kinds of customer segments involve expensive operations, both human and capital resources. An obvious potential here is using these collective facilities to increase risk pools so that the efficiency of risk management and pricing may be enhanced. Having the facility through a collective arrangement (helped by regulation) to take longer-term views on credit risk provisions for such customer segments might also be facilitated.

One possibility (not yet explored in detail to the authors' knowledge) is earmarking an element of 'social capital' (approved by regulators) within a bank's own capital adequacy resources that may be used to help neutralise part of the 'capital at risk' used in RAROC formulae for designated, higher risk, micro business borrowers. This 'social capital' quantum could be fixed by regulators as part of society's longer-term investment in developing otherwise excluded customer segments. Some related element of 'social' loan loss provisioning could also be considered in this kind of scheme. Such an approach would encompass both capital adequacy (downside risk) and loan loss provisioning (average risk) in a wider 'social capital quantum'. In this kind of system, moral hazard problems would have to be addressed. These kinds of moves, though, may eventually be needed in order to develop a more 'sustainable', longer-term attack on financial exclusion.

These kinds of collective approaches inevitably involve varying levels of Government action and regulation. This suggests the inevitability of some state control and direction in any co-ordinated (public/private) attack on financial exclusion, regeneration of marginalised geographic localities, financial education and the active development of an entrepreneurship strategy aimed at individuals and small businesses (microbusinesses). A private sector approach alone does not appear capable of delivering all of the sustained and longer-term benefits targeted. The government policy challenge has to be the protection of the free market model, whilst at the same time tackling financial exclusion in a sustained way.

At the same time, banking sectors can (and have) achieved a great deal towards overcoming financial exclusion. Much remains to be done. In the developing debate, 'social banking', 'regional banking', 'ethical banking', 'development banking' and 'community banking' are already being given a renewed emphasis. Institutions and concepts are clearly important. However, it is the fundamental economics reconciling these with legitimate and longer-term societal needs that lie at the heart of the evolving debate.

Bringing together economic (value-maximising) and social (welfare) objectives in this kind of model may not be so revolutionary as it might appear. European countries and the EU have adopted the free market and globalisation models. Historic political philosophies and related social welfare structures are now on the reform agenda. The objective will be to develop these in a more transparent, 'market-conformable' way. At the same time, we are entering an era of significant transformational change in bank regulation with the development of Basel 2. For the first time, the regulatory authorities are constructing a strong, comprehensive and general framework that integrates bank regulation (previously externally mandated by regulators) with free market discipline. The preceding proposals of designated 'social capital' quantums within a bank's capital adequacy resources could be argued to map into this kind of developing, more open and regulatory 'vicarious participation in management' philosophy. Requiring banks to disclose fully all of their regulatory designated social lending and investing specifically to help improve financial inclusion would be a necessary condition. For the moment, though, these kinds of proposals have to remain speculative.

In Spain, the savings banks have made a significant contribution towards reducing financial exclusion and this is of increasing strategic importance to them. Some examples of the savings banks' activities in this domain are summarised below:

- Geographical exclusion: Carbó, Rodríguez and López del Paso (2000) show that (in 2000) 3.45 per cent of the Spanish population are 'financially rescued' in the system because a savings bank has a branch (or several branches) in their town. In many small (low population density) towns, a savings bank is the only banking institution operating, thereby reducing the possibility of geographical financial exclusion.
- Socio-economic exclusion: A later study by Carbó and López del Paso (2002) shows that the economic profile of those towns 'rescued' from financial exclusion by savings bank presence are also characterised by low income levels and high unemployment.
- Ethnic exclusion: Many savings banks (of all sizes) have special schemes and products for immigrants. These include special savings accounts, specific money transfer instruments, micro-credit facilities and various other tailored products and services.
- Mortgage exclusion: Savings banks are very much involved in the subsidised mortgage rates programme that the Spanish Government offers to low-income families to buy a house. They also participate in one of the main public sector micro-credit initiatives through the state's Official Credit Institution. Both the subsidised mortgage rate and micro-credit programmes are also open to other financial institutions though the savings banks are particularly active in these schemes.

These select examples illustrate how the strategies and respective products and services of banks can play a key role in helping to tackle financial exclusion.

Up until now, we have seen that the banks in many countries have responded to the challenge of financial exclusion. British and French experiences (amongst others) also emphasise the role that the post office can play in this area. Pollin & Riva (2002, p. 235) make this point strongly and survey the recent experiences of the British and French post offices. The attraction of the post office network is its wide geographic coverage, penetration into regions and locales that are otherwise 'financially desertified', and their interface with poorer and otherwise disadvantaged members of society.

One of the key features of the Gothenburg conference (EC, 2001) was a kind of competition on ideas, products and services that help to improve financial exclusion. Three categories were covered:

- Insurance and savings;
- Credit services;
- Payment systems.

Around 150 banks, insurers, consumer, non-profit organisations and public bodies were invited to participate in the Gothenburg conference. In the end, 13 institutions participated. A jury of international experts evaluated the proposals using the following criteria:

- Outreach of the product, service or programme;
- Degree of innovation (relative to customer base);
- Organisational support;
- Target group;
- Social impact;
- Sustainability (for the customer);
- Degree of efficiency, profitability and sustainability (for the provider);
- Procedural efficiency.

Tables 7.1 and 7.2 provide a detailed overview of the results of this 'competition' and the respective products that were deemed most appropriate for combating exclusion.

The contribution of economic theory

Financial exclusion and the broader issue of social exclusion have been subject to an eclectic variety of research interests; economists, sociologists, political theorists, geographers, and strategists, to name but a few. Since financial exclusion is clearly a multi-disciplinary problem with many different aspects, this eclectic interest is understandable and

Table 7.1 Gothenburg (2000) competition on products to help combat financial exclusion

Credit services

Product group

Client orientation

| | | | | *Credit services* | |
| | | | | *Liquidity* | |

	Fundusz Mikro, Poland	First Step, Dublin, Ireland	VanCity, Canada	Finnvera Small Enterprises	WEETU (Women's Employment, Enterprise and Training Unit), Norwich, UK	Deutsche Ausgleichsbank (after a merger in 2003 noe part of KfW Mittelstandbank)
Organisation	http://www.funduszmikro.com.pl		http://www.vancity.com	http://www.finnvera.fi	http://www.weetu.org	http://www.kfw-mittelstandsbank.de
Product		First Step Micro Lending	Self Reliance Loans	Micro Loan	Full Circle Loan Fund	Round Table (management in crisis for SME)
Brief Description	Fundusz Micro offers unsecured loans to micro entrepreneurs without access to other external credit resources since 1994. It	Product is an unsecured and interest free loan including business advice with the aim to create employment	Micro-lending programme for new entrepreneurs and accessible to all members of VanCity, defined by membership in good standing	Micro loan and a special loan to women entrepreneurs for small start-up or existing businesses offering	Micro-credit available to women members since 1999. Self-ruled lending circles. Membership required to	Services offered: short-term consulting for small and medium-sized enterprises in crisis. Within 10 days an expert is

Table 7.1 Gothenburg (2000) competition on products to help combat financial exclusion *(continued)*

Credit services

Product group		Credit services			
Client orientation			*Liquidity*		
can be used for start-ups, for investments and for crises situations. The programme gained special importance after a massive flood in SW Poland in 1997 which, because of the lack of credit facilities, affected small business most severely. The guarantee provided relates to the co-signing within groups of at least four	through a new enterprise. Introduced in 1990. Elements of the micro lending programme are: Co-operation with mainstream banks (Bank of Ireland) and other financial institutions offers the chance to build a credit history. Purpose, term and repayment flexibility.	for at least six months. The loan can be offered as a term loan, a line of credit or as a combination of both. Four payments can be postponed in the first year, two payments in the following years. No fees charged. Maximum loan size has been $15,000 in the beginning, extended to $25,000 and $50,000 in exceptional cases.	employment to less than five people. Loan amount around Euro 3,000–32,000 Interest rate 6 months Euribor Service fee 2% (at least Euro 90) Maturity – 5 years and 1 years grace period.	obtain loan. Credit to self-employed women, mostly start-ups. First loan: up to £1000, maximum additional loan of £2000 area available if the first loan is repaid. The lending circle has always to agree. Circle members have to pay 5% of the loan into an emergency fund.	appointed to analyse the situation. Expert likely to recommend a reorganisation. The second stage includes a round table meeting with the expert as mediator, the entrepreneur, bank and other creditors. After care for 6 to 12 months after the crisis provided. Fees: short-term consulting fees.

Table 7.1 Gothenburg (2000) competition on products to help combat financial exclusion (*continued*)

Credit services

Product group	Credit services	
Client orientation	*Liquidity*	
members and each group member is usually a borrower and co-signer.	Networking to access additional funding where necessary.	Rate paid: base rate plus 1.5% (minimum 7.5%)
Limited formalities; loan application is only one sheet of paper.		Repayment: group liability (moral liability). No credit availability unless the circle has solved repayment problem.
Stable loan conditions for the entire loan repayment.		
Except for start-ups, business must be officially registered for at least three months and have the potential to be self-sufficient.		

Table 7.1 Gothenburg (2000) competition on products to help combat financial exclusion (*continued*)

Credit services

Product group

			Credit services			
Client orientation				*Liquidity*		
To what extent does the product differ from traditional services?	Loan granted for small amount, no security needed	Small amount, no security, high-risks	Loan granted despite high risks and low amount	Small credit amount Lower interest rates	Credit amount Business training and credit programme combined Networking idea/liability of a small group	Combination of assistance, empowerment of self-help, and attempt of a joint solution.
To what extent does the organisation play an innovative role out of its group?	Fundusz Mikro is the leading micro-credit group some Polish co-op banks are starting to offer similar services. Credit unions are entering the market. Co-op banks appear to charge less for their loans	No other financial institutions in Ireland offer any product similar.	No other financial institutions in the Vancouver area offer a similar product.	Finnerva is the only supplier of micro loans in Finland.	Combination of training, aftercare, networking and financing. An innovative general (economic) approach.	To be aware of the entrepreneur's general situation and not a single (economic) problem.

Table 7.1 Gothenburg (2000) competition on products to help combat financial exclusion (*continued*)

Credit services				
Product group	*Credit services*			
Client orientation	*Liquidity*			
Does the product have an innovative effect in the service branch concerned?		Job creation effect. After the initial success of the programme there has been co-operation with the Federal Department of Western Economic Diversification that now pursues similar lending programmes with other credit unions in Canada.		Social responsibility in the local area. dea of mediation land partnership among all parties involved.
How much is the target group excluded from financial services?	Micro-entrepreneurs to a large extent have no access to any credit facility. Formal requirements and procedures are too onerous.	Participants excluded because risks are too high and income too low.	Many participants rely on unemployment insurance payments and are marginalised in the community as a whole.	Difficulties to get suitable credit.	No access to traditional credit. Most participants have been employed for more than two years. Exclusion of women from financial services

Table 7.1 Gothenburg (2000) competition on products to help combat financial exclusion (*continued*)

Credit services			
Product group	*Credit services*		
Client orientation	*Liquidity*		
	Participants excluded from traditional credit services because they are too high risk and lack income.	is a special problem.	Long-term support (including start-up and development period). Idea of networking, group responsibility, mentoring.	Quick non-bureaucratic help by experts.
How appropriate is the product for the target group's central needs?	Credit facilities are of main importance for entrepreneurs. Loan process designed to meet the needs of a micro business.	While offering means of self reliance, it addresses the central reason for financial exclusion.	Addresses financial exclusion for unemployed people.	
How strong is the qualitative impact for the social	Beyond the general effects, the free membership in	The product has helped build networking of new entrepreneurs	Collective level: mutual support and trust, active problem solving	A large number of enterprises could be stabilised.

Table 7.1 Gothenburg (2000) competition on products to help combat financial exclusion (*continued*)

	Credit services			
Product group				
Client orientation		*Liquidity*		
framework with regard to access?	the Small Firms Association, networking support and co-operation with a mainstream Bank promote re-integration of customers.	and training service provides which results in annual award nights that recognise business achievements.		and 'building social capital'. Individual level: increasing confidence, empowerment, improved knowledge (financial literacy, debt management).
Does the product depend on public subsidies, and if yes, how transparent and efficient are these integrated?	The Polish American Enterprise Fund set up $20 million to be used for the programme.	Subsidies from the private sector, EU Government and major financial institutions. Donations from private and corporate sector amount to £2 million. Budget deficits are underwritten.	No, except a loan loss reserve is provided by the partner Federal Department of Western Economic Diversification.	Finnerva is state owned.	'External subsidies' (i.e. credit from the Charities Aid Foundation guaranteed with a grant from NatWest bank, running costs are met by charitable donations and local government funding)

Table 7.1 Gothenburg (2000) competition on products to help combat financial exclusion (continued)

Credit services					
Product group			*Credit services*		
Client orientation			*Liquidity*		
Does the programme cover its operational costs?	Yes	(see above)	Yes		
How many clients does the programme reach?	For 1998/99: 10,240 clients, total loans $17.8 million. / Since inception: 34,245 and $58 million in loans	May 1998 – May 1999 more than 500 people approached First Step. In 1999, 153 loans issued to Euro 776,000. Since 1990 more than 850 new businesses have been funded with a loan amount of Euro 4 million	700 clients since 1996 with a total loan amount of $7.5 million, in 1999 184 participants.	The programme has existed since 1996/7. About 3,000 clients within the last year (loans admitted Euro 130,000)	January 1999 to May 2000: 80 women have formed 17 lending circles; 26 loans have been made totalling £15,747,1005 repayment). 620 enquiries and about 200 joined interviews or meetings.

Table 7.1 Gothenburg (2000) competition on products to help combat financial exclusion *(continued)*

Credit services				
Product group			*Credit services*	
Client orientation			*Liquidity*	
Which region does the programme cover in relation to its clients served?	Throughout Poland	Throughout Ireland	In Greater Vancouver	Finland and International	Norfolk, UK

Source: Adapted from Gothenburg (2000) Conference 'Competition on Products to Help Combat Financial Exclusion', various tables

Table 7.2 Gothenburg (2000) competition on products to help combat financial exclusion – Payment and savings services

Product group	Means of payment		Insurance and savings	No access/wrong target group		
Client orientation	Liquidity		Liquidity			
Organisation	Bank of Scotland	Stadtspakasee Koln	Cambridge Housing Society (CHS) and Cambridge Building Society	GLS Geneinschatsbank eG	Okobank	Irish Banks & Building Societies
Product	Current account for financially excluded	Basic banking service	New Horizons Saving and Loan Scheme	Lending and Donation Communities	Socially and/or ecologically innovative services	Paymaster (education programme)
Brief Description	Easycash account – is a money transmission account that allows access to the banking to the financially excluded. Day-to-day finances can be managed without a cheque book and credit	Product provides basic banking services (during 1995 especially to recipients of social assistance, now to all consumers without account including minors) by opening a 'Mindestgirokonto'. Installation of	Financial services for CHS tenants (including family members). Offers affordable loans and saving accounts for CHS tenants and families. Savings account	To serve a special social purpose (i.e. sponsoring of a local school, financial support of family, expansion of a local business) a self-governed 'Lending and Donation Community' (for a maximum	Financing products since 1988 for projects with an 'socially and/or ecologically innovative approach' in the following areas: environment and energy; women; psychiatry, self-employment	Education programme (introduced 1997) assisting teachers in their business lessons for (young) students. Covers: understanding and utilising payments systems, personal financial

Table 7.2 Gothenburg (2000) competition on products to help combat financial exclusion – Payment and savings services *(continued)*

Product group	Means of payment		Insurance and savings	No access/wrong target group		
	facilities. The account has Keycard facilities at over 20,000 cash machines, and includes the ability to pay by Solo in shops and offers phoneline facilities. There are no account charges. Counter transactions are charged £1 to encourage ATM use. A £10 buffer ensures the withdrawal of the last £ if necessary via ATM.	ATM's at local social security offices and a special weekly consultation service.	(maximum £10,000) with enhanced interest rates. Loan accounts with low interest rates (for borrowing prior savings are required). Maximum first loan £1,000 (for subsequent loan £2,000). Interest rate: base rate plus 0.95%, repayment period is 2 years. Trial period (end of 2000): handy loan account with no prior savings	period of five years) will be established (i.e. teachers and parents will establish a community to support their school). Members commit themselves to contribute a special amount in favour of the Community. For this each Community member applies for a micro credit (limit Euro 5,000). GLS passes the total amount of all micro credits to the	and social commitment. Products have generally favourable conditions: lower interest rates. Products include loans, saving bonds, closed-end funds and others especially networking and know-how support.	management and budgeting. There are four main elements: video on key money management concepts; teacher notes; examples of credit and debit cards; cheque book. Produced by the Irish Bankers Federation in consultation with Business Studies Teachers Association of Ireland and other similar associations.

Table 7.2 Gothenburg (2000) competition on products to help combat financial exclusion – Payment and savings services (continued)

Product group	Means of payment	Insurance and savings	No access/wrong target group
			Target group: post primary students (12–18 years, divided into three groups) with Business studies as subject. Material is free of charge.
	necessary, maximum amount of loan £150, repayment period is 12 months.		Community as earmarked donations. The Community has thereby already sufficient own capital funds at the start of the project. Credit repayment: no interest rate but costs (around Euro 80), joint liability of the Community members.
		Higher interest rates on savings.	GLS accepts its social responsibility. Idea of a collective account. No interest rate. Favourable conditions for socially and/or ecologically innovative projects.
To what extent does the product differ from traditional services?	In traditional British financial services, people without a certain credit rating or sufficient identification papers have not received current account facilities.	Just a deposit account. Special consultation services for low income consumers.	Traditional banking information with no marketing elements.

Table 7.2 Gothenburg (2000) competition on products to help combat financial exclusion – Payment and savings services *(continued)*

Product group	Means of payment		Insurance and savings	No access/wrong target group		
Does the product have an innovative effect in the service branch concerned?	Similar products offered by competitors. Charges originally made for use of competitors ATM's have been dropped.	Positively demonstrates the connection between exclusion of financial services and exclusion from society.	Other local associations asked for similar joint ventures with CHS and CBS.	The idea of 'Community of Solidarity' and a partnership between Community, its members and financing bank.		Responsible for financial literacy of the younger generation.
How much is the target group excluded from financial services?	Access to most financial services presupposes a current account. Those without such accounts are excluded.	Recipients of social assistance are often confronted with the termination of their current accounts or the refusal of re-opening such accounts.	Difficulties to get affordable credits or to open a bank account.	The reason for the Communities' establishment is lack of own capital with the result of insufficient creditworthiness for traditional banks.	Not generally excluded though market conditions may often defer success of projects.	It is not.
How appropriate is the product for the target group's central needs?	Provides a basic payments tool.	Access to basic financial services is important for financially excluded.	High demand for services reflecting need.		Offers means of financing.	Difficult to say as programme is focused on teachers' needs.

Table 7.2 Gothenburg (2000) competition on products to help combat financial exclusion – **Payment and savings services** *(continued)*

Product group	Means of payment	Insurance and savings	No access/wrong target group
Does the programme cover its operational costs?	No information, but cost kept low by automation.		Does return match investment – No / Yes
How many clients does the programme reach?	Not available	1999: 28,000 accounts / October 1997 to May 1999: 58 savings accounts with a combined sum of £21,000 saved. 35 loan accounts (25 handy loans)	Programme has existed since 1974. Around 50 new Communities established every year with a total volume of Euro 2.2 million per year. / Okobank has 33,000 customers. / 1999: 300 schools.
Which region does the programme cover in relation to its clients served?	Easycash is available in all Bank of Scotland branches (Note: Bank of Scotland merged with Halifax and is now part of the HBOS group / Cologne and surrounding area.	Cambridge and surrounding area.	National / Germany / Republic of Ireland

Source: see Table 7.1

appropriate. 'Institutionalist' and 'behavioural' may best describe the kind of economics domain that would appear to be needed in order to develop any kind of overall 'theory of financial exclusion'. This is not our present concern. Nor are we concerned for the moment with the increasing importance of 'rule of thumb' economies in macroeconomic economic models and how financial exclusion studies may help to inform these issues.[1]

Our present concern is pragmatic. We focus on how economic theory may be able to help explain why financial exclusion occurs and, in doing so, provide some practical insight into how the banking system ('bank strategies') might be developed to combat it. To this end, we explore the following areas:

- Bank strategies that flow from the 'free market model' (and the consequences of shareholder value maximisation and variants of it);
- Asymmetric information (the extent to which financial exclusion is an information problem);
- Statistical discrimination (and related techniques, like credit scoring);
- The role of financial development in regional development (which is related to the problem of 'financial desertification').

We begin with the economics of the free market model.

Throughout this study we have at various points discussed the impact of the free market, the ubiquitous 'shareholder wealth maximisation' (SWM) model, on financial exclusion. In this context, US and UK experiences are likely to provide a good insight (allowing for institutional differences between countries) of likely development paths in Europe. Indeed, we can already see developing similarities between US and UK experiences.

Deregulation and the rise of the SWM model appear, at one level, to increase financial inclusion. More financial products are supplied in response to (actual and perceived) market demand than before. At the same time, however, the rise of risk-based pricing, related techniques like RORAC and increasing pressures to be more productively efficient (reduce costs) *inter alia* conspire to focus banks' strategic emphasis more on certain customer groups, rather than on customers in general.

---

[1] The potential relevance of financial exclusion studies in this domain were suggested by Professor Jordi Gali at a workshop organised in Salamanca by the Spanish Savings Banks in July 2004.

In particular, 'valuable' customer groups are targeted, those that help to increase a bank's 'value-added' in a SWM sense. As Boyce (2000, p. 649) summarises the process: 'Customer valuation is shown to have become a means to increase shareholder income and wealth, almost inevitably at the cost of (further) marginalising the poor and disadvantaged'.

This deregulation (*de facto* and *de jure*) induced process, then, appears to exacerbate financial exclusion. At the same time financial crises (another apparent feature of modern financial systems) attenuate this process. Financial crises appear to be a feature of the present development of financial systems. This may, of course, be the transition phase (of some considerable duration) towards some higher order, deregulated and 'complete' set of financial markets that is free of present 'market failures' (like the 'Too big to fail' doctrine and the lack of a global market in bank corporate control). Whatever the likely or hypothesised duration (or even existence) of such a transition phase, recurring financial crises appear to be characteristic of the present financial and economic era.

Whenever there is a financial crisis, there is invariably an aftermath of some kind of 'flight to quality' and an emphasis on risk reduction by the banking and financial services industry. Leyshon and Thrift (1993, p. 223) describe the resultant effects as ... 'abandonment and retreat to a more affluent client base'. This applies not only to particular customer segments, but also to respective geographic localities (so-called 'financial desertification'). Leyshon and Thrift (1995, p. 312) further characterise the economic process as ... 'increasingly exclusionary in response to a financial crisis founded in higher levels of competition and extreme levels of indebtedness'.

Dymski and Li (2002) show in the geographic literature that in modern US banking, financial exclusion is typically linked to a particular set of macrostructural circumstances. In the present context, though, Dymski and Li confirm (2002, p. 1): 'Certainly, one impetus for changes in banking strategy and hence for financial exclusion is the enhanced financial competition triggered by globalisation and deregulation'. They go on to argue from their research that not all banks have followed the lead of the megabanks in their 'strategic shift' towards emphasising higher value customers.

This latter 'strategic shift' (the apparent industry norm) is associated *inter alia* with a growing separation between the financial circumstances and options of lower-income and higher-income households. Much of the latter group now have instantaneous access to financial information, transactions and value transfers of their wealth, present and prospective. This emergent status of 'global financial citizenship' has given these societal groups a new kind of power. As a source of already assured 'value additivity' and known risk, this group is also increasingly targeted by the main commercial banks.

This enhanced power is in marked contrast to those lower-income groups at the other end of the household spectrum. These 'un-banked' or 'marginally banked' groups apparently have less information about products, are not so heavily (if at all) targeted for new products and the dynamics of this bank strategic process appear to exacerbate this inherent polarisation. We have already discussed how key bank strategic drivers like deregulation, intensifying competition, globalisation and modern financial crises seem to exacerbate financial exclusion in the 'free market mode'. Other key drivers are securitisation and retail disintermediation.

Securitisation is the shifting of credit intermediation (primarily by the corporate sector) out of the banking system into capital markets. Retail disintermediation describes the shift of savings out of the banking system into money-market mutual funds and offshore vehicles; this process restricts the lending investment capacity of the banking system. Securitisation, on the other hand, reduces the corresponding demand for commercial bank lending. On the one hand, these trends have emphasised the development of investment banking and asset management strategies by US banks. At the same time, they have stimulated banks to re-examine their core banking business. In particular, the banks have sought new ways to 'lock in' their customers and make more profit ('value added') from them.

New kinds of deposit instruments, moving into new areas of lending, increasing use of ABS (Asset-backed Securities) techniques in lending, improving risk management and risk-mitigation techniques, and a generalised movement towards risk-based pricing characterise this new strategic environment. Dymski and Li (2002, p. 4) emphasise that from a customer perspective, 'standardisation' has been integral in these renewed US banking strategies in consumer banking. This process of standardisation is further attenuated by an increasing use of computer-based technology to assess credit risks, inform loan selection and direct pricing. Local knowledge of staff and discretion become less important, a process further emphasised as the SWM model stimulates banks to reduce their staffing (and branching) levels in the search for ever greater cost efficiency. Standardised (profitable) customers can be more easily targeted for cross-selling a bank's existing and new products; standardised loans are more easily originated and securitised.

In this new, post-deregulation US market, banks' strategies, then, have been directed towards searching for profitable 'standardised' customers. These latter customer groups can be targeted in several, non mutually-exclusive ways. For example, lower profit customer groups can be nurtured and helped to grow by the bank's; customer groups may be sought in new geographic locations; and/or a bank may merge with another bank(s). The latter is often the fastest way to achieve the desired result and helps to explain the US bank merger wave of recent years and the growing dominance of banking markets by a few megabanks.

Dymski and Li (2002, p. 5) emphasise that in modern US banking... 'mergers and acquisitions are central to the dynamic of the standardised customer'. They characterise pre-deregulation US banking as relatively low fixed banking costs and high marginal costs of servicing customers. The post-deregulation phase, the new megabanking, is an era of high fixed costs (of product design, testing and marketing) and low marginal costs of servicing customers. The basic target is to pursue the more profitable customer groups, develop these customer relationships through time and to target them increasingly for a wider range of 'value-adding' products.

The basic economics of this process, then, suggest that the mainstream commercial banks increasingly 'desert' the less profitable household groups. Since these latter, poorer groups are often clustered in particular geographical locales (parts of a city or a region), the resultant financial exclusion has an inevitable geographic (as well as social and economic) spatial dimension. We have also seen earlier that where mainstream financial services are not available, other alternatives can and do develop to 'fill the gaps'. Nevertheless, this kind of 'financial desertification' may constrain continued economic and financial development activities. Dymski and Li (2002) posit whether ethnobanking experiences in Los Angeles (under very special macrostructural conditions) suggest a possible alternative to financial exclusion (or, instead, are merely 'the exception that proves the rule').

US and UK experiences, then, with the post-deregulation 'free market model' appear to provide some interesting, though disturbing insights. The main message seems to be that the free market model, by itself, may exacerbate the problem of financial exclusion. At the very least, it appears to increase the polarisation of financially included and excluded societal groups. At worst the free market model may also increase the numbers (sub-segments) of groups excluded as risk-based pricing becomes more sophisticated. As with competition, the free market model unchecked is not a solution. Some kind of 'intervention' and 'partnership approach' to financial exclusion is apparently needed. 'Intervention' in this context is any set of actions that an unregulated private sector firm would not normally undertake. Such actions range from government edicts (affirmative action), government as mediator to 'self regulation' by the industry itself.

'Self regulation' in this context covers those banking sub-sectors (whether privately, mutually or state-owned) whose primary mission was the development of their regions, helping poorer sectors of the customer-base and aiding social works. Many such institutions have undoubtedly been driven towards more profit, greater efficiency and product portfolios similar to their commercial bank competitors. In the modern era, though, the longer-term commercial viability of such banks' initial strategic objectives remains an open question. As we saw in the last section, society at large and government may now be required to make a more positive investment in such socially and economically desirable policies. For the present, though, we move to the second of our economic areas of concern, asymmetric information.

The modern economic rationale for banks and banking is explained largely in the corpus of information economics. A basic problem of information economics is that of asymmetric information. The latter occurs when one party to a product being transacted (like a potential borrower asking for a bank loan) has more information that the other (the potential lender). Whenever these conditions exist, problems like adverse selection and moral hazard arise. If these problems are not handled appropriately, more risky and destabilising transactions will increasingly dominate. In modern financial systems, banks exist as one of the most efficient mechanisms to date of assessing, evaluating and monitoring credit risks. Banks are viewed as 'delegated monitors' (of their depositors) who provide 'signals' to financial markets about the creditworthiness of borrowers. Banks are not the only means of reducing asymmetric information problems (others include techniques like regulation, collateral and net worth), but they are seen economically as especially important in this process (Mishkin, 1997).

This important economics literature used in explaining modern banking may also be directly relevant to the problems of financial exclusion. The question becomes whether financial exclusion is 'explained' simply by asymmetric information. Put simply, are the financially excluded the result of the banks not having adequate information upon which to construct accurate risk and return-based prices? The latter include any relevant credit risk mitigation techniques that might be feasible and economic to deploy if the full credit risk profile of the borrower was known *ex ante* to the bank.

There are at least two possible conjectures one might raise. One is that banking markets are inefficient in this world because of asymmetric information between the banks and potential borrowers, the financially excluded. This is the kind of argument advanced by Rothschild and Stiglitz (1976) in a celebrated article on the insurance market. They demonstrate in this context that insurance markets are 'pareto inefficient': that is, someone amongst parties in this market can be made better off without making anyone worse off and the insurance market fails to impound this potential gain because the participants do not have the complete information. A simple, two-person game theory model is used by Broome (1989) to give the same result: see also Chakravarty (2004b).

These theoretical results appear to confirm that asymmetric information between the banks and the financially excluded can be a potentially serious problem. Of course, there are some complex theoretical and practical (our main concern) problems. An obvious practical problem is who should bear the 'search and monitoring' costs of closing this information gap? In helping to relieve financial exclusion, better and more complete information ('costly state verification') about the financially excluded are obvious desiderata; they are also likely to be relatively expensive. There is clearly an 'information gap' between banks and the financially excluded. Our survey also suggests that a corresponding information gap also exists on the impact of various bank moves to help overcome financial exclusion.

Another problem (theoretical, but with a clear practical consequence) is that what might be in the best, profit-maximising interest of an individual bank may not necessarily be in the value-maximising interest of society ('the world') at large: this kind of problem is well known in the international flow of capital and related bank regulation literature: see for example, Kim (1993, chs. 2 & 12). These are all important theoretical and policy concerns. There is also a lack of data in these key domains. But these considerations also lead us to our third area of concern, the possibility of statistical discrimination.

Do present credit scoring models of potential bank borrowers effectively discriminate against certain groups of customers because of 'information deficiency' or 'imperfect efficiency' in the words of Rothschild and Stiglitz (1976)? This is of direct practical concern in the present context and it is explored by Chakravarty (2004a & b).

The argument runs like this: the dynamics in the banking industry released by deregulation and other free market forces are inherently beneficial to society since they ultimately make the system more efficient (in a SWM sense) than before. Bigger banks, more concentrated banking systems, staff cuts and branch closures are all a natural part of this same, 'value-enhancing' process. This latter process and related trends, like staff cuts and branch closures, are also facilitated by technological advances. These not only help to improve a bank's risk management capabilities, they also render the geographical location of a branch less relevant. Data can be gathered, stored and processed 'at a distance'. As a result of all these developments, banks are generally more efficient (a good thing) and no customers should be disadvantaged by the resultant branch and staff cut-backs in some locales (since technology can do all of the things 'at a distance' and at a lower cost than branches and staff could do before 'on the ground').

The concern in this world is that customers in the 'desertified' areas will be discriminated against on the basis of their geographic location. This is a different kind of discrimination than that of statistical discrimination on the basis of the creditworthiness of applicants (rather than on their location *per se*). The latter is presumably 'acceptable' in this world in that it is based on objective, market-determined criteria and such discrimination is the price of economic efficiency. Discrimination on the basis of geographic location, however, is not well-founded in this sense: it comes closer to 'redlining' and other, more dubious forms of discrimination. Chakravarty (2004a) argues that theory, supported by survey evidence, suggests that personal contacts (branch and lending officer proximity) play an information-processing role (of so-called 'soft information') in the provision of credit and other financial services. In short, the quality of information that banks use in processing lending requests in peripheral areas would be enhanced if the banks were engaged more (in closer physical proximity) with these areas. In this kind of lending, 'knowing the local market' and 'knowing your applicant' are, by definition, even more crucial.

To summarise, 'discrimination' in bank lending on business criteria is the result of value-maximising behaviour by banks. In itself, this is the result of business necessity; it does not reflect any kind of prejudice (in a 'redlining' sense). This kind of lending activity, though, may well exacerbate the peripheral nature of the regional economy. Technology may also help to facilitate this same economic process.

However, Chakravarty's (2000a) work emphasises that information may become 'noisier' under these circumstances as banks cut back on their branches and staff. There seems to be good grounds for believing that this is a real problem, although it remains to be tested statistically. For example, Berger *et al* (2004) review the literature on bank lending to SMEs and confirm *inter alia* that big banks (who lend at greater distances) have a comparative disadvantage in extending relationship credit to SMEs. This kind of phenomenon may increase the apparent riskiness of lending to some household groups and smaller firms. Chakravarty (2004a, p. 27) emphasises the need for government ... 'to encourage organisational forms that have a stake in the local community'. He also emphasises the need for public action aimed at encouraging and nurturing such institutions. The need for better quality and more detailed information on regions and the impact of bank lending in such regions are also underscored.

The empirical evidence on the kind of specific issues that we have just discussed is quite 'spotty' and heavily US-orientated. Avery *et al* (2004) examine the potential costs of not incorporating situational data into consumer credit evaluations; these kinds of data include the economic environment in which consumers live or work. The empirical tests of Avery *et al* (2004) produce strong inferences that situational circumstances influence an individual's propensity to default on a new loan. Berger *et al* (2002) examine the economic effects of small business credit scoring (SBCS). Their findings *inter alia* suggest that SBCS may allow some large banks to expand their lending to at least some pools of small businesses. They also ask the question whether small US banks have lost an important comparative advantage to large banks because of SBCS. In a later study, Berger *et al* (2004) review the literature and confirm that the data from developed countries generally support the view that large banks are 'disadvantaged' in SME lending: that is, they allocate a much lower proportion of their assets to SME loans than do small banks. Clearly, more detailed and extended research into these kinds of areas is needed in Europe.

The final area that we noted at the start of this section is the role of financial development (and different kinds of financial development) in regional economic re-generation. The link between financial and economic growth is the subject of extensive theoretical and empirical testing. Al-Yousif (2002), for example, finds that financial development and economic growth are mutually causal in developing countries. His results also support the World Bank (and others) view that the relationship between economic growth and financial development cannot be generalised across countries because economic policies tend to be country specific.

At regional and bank lending levels, the empirical literature (especially European) is more sparse. Carbó Valverde and Rodríguez Fernández (2004) examined a sample of Spanish banks during 1993–1999 and found that economic growth predicted financial deepening at a regional level during this period. They also found that bank lending specialisation appears to be a key issue in financial regional growth compared with other kinds of bank specialisation. In an international analysis of community banking and economic performance, Berger *et al* (2004) found that greater market shares and efficiency ranks of small, private and domestically-owned banks are associated with better economic performance. In this study, they focus on one dimension of the financial system, the health of community banks relative to other banks and how this impacts on the economy.

Conclusions

This chapter has synthesised and summarised some key aspects of the developing European scenario for financial exclusion. The developing European government policy responses confirm that financial exclusion is an increasingly important area. Already many banks and banking sectors have begun to develop various responses to these challenges. Finally, we explored the contribution and role of economic and related empirical testing. Our conclusion here was that there is considerable scope and a practical need for more research related to the study of financial exclusion so as to help inform the policy debate.[2]

---

[2] A major international conference hosted by the World Bank and the World Savings Banks Institute, held in Brussels, in October 2004 re-affirmed the increasing importance and policy concern with financial exclusion. (WSBI and the World Bank, 2004).

8
Financial Exclusion in Developing Countries

Introduction

This chapter examines issues relating to financial exclusion in developing countries. There are many parallels between initiatives being made in the developed and developing world to encourage parts of society to make greater use of financial services. Obviously, many developing countries have substantially underdeveloped financial institutions and systems with a much greater part of the population having no financial services. The chapter focuses on the main features of financial exclusion in developing countries and examines various mechanisms that have been suggested to promote financial inclusion covering the role of informal financial networks and various microfinance initiatives. Reference throughout the chapter is made to the broader finance and development literature that also emphasises the promotion of the financial services industry as an important driver of economic growth.

Features of financial exclusion in developing countries

The problem of financial exclusion is clearly different in industrialised and developing countries at least, for two main reasons:

- Financial exclusion in developing countries affects the vast majority of the population and it is strongly related to poverty and the absence of capital resources. As a consequence, there is a complete set of institutional factors that should be considered as sources of financial exclusion in these countries; and
- Developing countries exhibit a significantly lower level of financial development compared to industrialised economies. Therefore,

financial exclusion in these countries is associated with financial underdevelopment and it is necessary to demonstrate the importance of finance for growth and poverty alleviation.

According to Holden and Prokopenko (2001) various sources of financial underdevelopment can be identified both from the public and private sides. From the government perspective, the state-owned model of financial system tends to dominate in most developing countries. In this context, there have been several episodes of political opportunistic behaviour that have resulted in an unequal distribution of resources. Typically, market-based incentive schemes that have been incorporated into state-dominated financial systems have not operated properly, since politicians have been unable to find the adequate mechanisms to encourage the managers of state-owned financial institutions to run banks and other financial firms in an efficient manner.

The regulatory issues are also of importance in evaluating the role of the government in financial underdevelopment. First of all, the financial architecture of many developing countries is deficient. Many of the basic elements of modern financial systems – such as entry requirements to the banking sectors, deposit insurance, functional separation of financial institutions, solvency regulations or lender of last resort facilities – have not been yet implemented in these countries. Besides, Holden and Prokopenko (2001) have also demonstrated that the reliance on direct instruments of monetary policy (control of interest rates) has also been harmful for credit provision and financial development. The move towards indirect instruments (such as open market operations or reserve requirements), however, in many countries during the last two decades has been proved to be less repressive for financial development.

With regards the private sector, the role of financial institutions is particularly relevant in developing countries, considering the exclusive dependence (when available) of most households and firms on bank financing and the absence of alternatives in the capital markets. It should be noted that the traditional monitoring and screening functions of financial intermediaries is difficult to implement in these economies, due to the absence of efficient information mechanisms and a very limited range of investment projects and/or guarantees/ collateral. Therefore, the adverse selection problem becomes central in many developing country financial systems since 'insiders' (depositors) do not have incentives to behave prudently.

The relatively low level of savings in developing countries and the inability of financial institutions to collect them properly is also a major problem. It is worth noting – also from the supply side – that many financial institutions do not operate with the appropriate technological capacity to enjoy scale economies and expand their branch networks. As a result, the difficulties (or even reluctance) of the population to open a current or savings account is not surprising. All in all, the low level of financial intermediary development in these countries can be explained by an inefficient supply of services, an insufficient demand and a high degree of self-exclusion related to the untrustworthiness of potential depositors in the whole system.

There are also other sources of inefficiencies in the banking sectors of developing countries associated with inappropriate management and regulatory frameworks. First of all, loan provision is directly affected by the inability of banks to manage credit risk. This inability is largely associated with macroeconomic instability. This situation may result in credit rationing, when banks do not lend to low quality borrowers. Alternatively, if lending is excessive, default rates can increase substantially, which, in turn, will worsen the macroeconomic situation. Information problems are also exacerbated due to the existence – in most of the banking sectors of developing countries – of poor accounting records that hampers credit risk management. The absence of adequate management control across bank branch networks – when managers in the head office do not have control of individual decisions at the branch level – also imply inefficiencies in credit risk assessment. Besides, it is difficult to rely on collateral since households in many developing countries do not have adequate property rights that provide them with a secure title to their property.

Rural economies and financial underdevelopment

One of the key elements of financial exclusion in developing countries is the existence of a rural-based socio-economic structure. Therefore, the geography of financial exclusion is again affected by the characteristics of the rural environment and all the institutional, regulatory and microeconomic issues of financial underdevelopment need to be assessed in this context.

Wenner (2000) surveys the problems of financial development and financial exclusion in rural areas following the lessons of several experiences at the Inter-American Development Bank. Several problems are identified that may be of use in identifying the sources of financial exclusion in these countries. Three of the sources of financial underdevelopment are particularly relevant to financial exclusion: pricing and risk behaviour in financial intermediation; information asymmetries; and transaction costs associated with the institutional setting. First of all, as far as pricing and risk behaviour are concerned, rural economies are marked by high risk techniques. Rural agricultural entrepreneurs – mostly individual or small firm groups – usually undertake financial contracts that are subject to a high degree of (economic) variability and usually result in involuntary default. There are various sources of variability at this level: supply variability from unfavourable production conditions (weather, disease, health conditions, equipment failure), variability in input prices that increase costs of production or changes in supply arising from altered price expectations.

Households and firms in rural areas follow various strategies that aim to tackle these problems. First of all, they can invest in social collateral to generate credit availability from informal sources such as Rotating Saving and Credit Associations (ROSCA's). ROSCA's are one of the most developed informal financial institutions in developing countries, and are used widely in Africa and Asia. The main principle of ROSCA's is almost the same everywhere – a group of individuals gather for a series of meetings and at each meeting everybody contributes to a common pot. The pot is given to one member of the group and this member is then excluded from receiving the pot in the future meetings while still contributing to the pot. The process is repeated until every member receives the pot. Once all members have received the pot then the ROSCA's is disbanded or it may start another cycle.

Lower availability of credit hinders diversification and increases vulnerability to risk. Another source of risk in rural economies is the limited set of default risk mitigation mechanisms, such as collateral, that are available. The latter implies a risk premium in the interest charged on credit. It is also difficult to set up adequate loan loss reserves systems. Overall, the limited geographic coverage of financial intermediation coupled with the fact that many of the economic activities (on which finance is to be provided) are interrelated and this reduces risk diversification. Subsequently, opportunities for profitable intermediation are reduced. Therefore, formal intermediaries do not seem to have incentives to penetrate rural markets.

Information asymmetries are also particularly relevant in rural markets. The cost of obtaining and processing information are also central in assessing and managing risk. Considering the abovementioned problems associated with risks, additional information about borrower quality can mitigate screening, adverse selection, and moral hazard problems to a certain extent. In most rural settings, social collateral (reputation) is employed as a substitute for real collateral. These tied relationships are relevant for agents such as ROSCA's, village banks and traditional moneylenders. These (informal) intermediaries obtain information about the creditworthiness of customers more rapidly and at lower cost than a formal intermediary. Consequently, informal lenders can more accurately identify those clients who will repay a loan commitment as long as the project return or household resources permit. From the demand side, depositors have similar problems since it is difficult for them to trust the fiduciary capacity of these intermediaries.

Monitoring is another element in the puzzle of information asymmetries in rural areas once screening has been completed. As any other financial intermediary, rural lenders should invest in monitoring the behaviour of clients to avoid moral hazard incentive problems. However, there appear scale diseconomies associated with this process since formal financial intermediaries find these monitoring costs unbearable, considering the small size of loans demanded by most rural customers. As a result, contracts based on reputation and social proximity constitute the main substitute for formal monitoring in these areas.

The third factor associated with financial exclusion in rural areas of developing countries is the role of transaction costs and the institutional setting. As opposed to high-income clients in developed countries, the significantly low level of income and the greater degree of spatial dispersion of rural clients in developing countries results in higher transaction costs for both intermediaries and customers. Transaction costs in rural areas are particularly affected by some of the main institutional factors, including property rights, contract enforcement, and prudential regulation and supervision.[1]

In rural areas, the absence or inefficiency of legal frameworks that secure property rights is particularly problematic. Strongly related to property rights themselves, contract enforcement represent all sorts of legal and social claims against property, including debtor's property – complete definition and control of the property – and security interest – which are the rights to be paid from the sale or exchange of the

---

[1] See Demirgüç-Kunt and Maksimovic (1998) for a survey of the implications of different legal and financial environments for economic development in both developed and developing countries.

property. However, most of the land or/and property registries in developing countries are deficient and make searching, registering, and documenting security interest expensive, time consuming, and risky. In this context, lending against accounts receivable is too risky as lenders cannot rely on public registries to learn if another creditor has a prior claim.

Prudential regulations and supervision are also deficient as a mechanism to correct or mitigate market failure arising from moral hazard and informational asymmetries between suppliers and consumers of financial services. Structural controls, prudential norms, and consumer protection regulations are the three main areas that define the problem of banking sector and financial system supervision in developing countries and, particularly, in rural areas. Structural controls refer to market entry and exit, geographic restrictions, consolidation and the range of services that financial firms can offer. Prudential controls seek to provide stability to the system by making individual financial institutions safer, thereby increasing consumer confidence. Consumer protection regulations are related to information disclosure and the development of systems for the resolution of disputes. However, the information provided is not always easy to interpret (nor to compare) due to different accounting standards employed in developing countries. This creates non-transparency for regulators, shareholders, and depositors. Rules on capital adequacy standards, accounting reforms and provisioning requirements have been implemented in many developing countries, although there is still a long way ahead for improvements on stability. Why are these problems particularly relevant in rural areas? Again, the answer is strongly related to the institutional environment.

Considering the characteristics of rural economies, the existence of specialised financial institutions that efficiently develop screening and monitoring functions in rural activities is a key issue. Although some developing countries allow the existence of financial institutions with a narrow range of services, many legal frameworks do not allow specialised or narrow banking. Other countries require high minimum capital standards that favour the creation of a small number of financial entities as opposed to a multitude with low standards. These requirements increase consolidation in the banking sector and worsen competition, specialisation and the geographic dispersion of financial services.

As an alternative, many types of semi-formal entities (credit unions, village banks, and cooperatives) or informal entities (supplier-traders, ROSCA's, and moneylenders) have flourished in these rural environments while formal financial institutions are not so common. Instead of providing multiple individual loans, the use of group credit has become common for these institutions, which seems to be more appropriate for collateral constrained borrowers. Considering this structure, transactions size are generally the lowest for informal providers, slightly higher for semi-formal entities, and the highest for formal financial intermediaries. However, as Wenner (2000) points out, after a number of cycles, transaction costs can increase substantially in group credit schemes and it may become necessary to provide individual loan products to keep the customer base. The main reason is the existence of mismatches between client needs and products offered that generate additional transaction costs and inefficiencies.

The benefits attributed to informal intermediaries – such as supplier-traders, ROSCA's, and moneylenders – are information advantages due to proximity, deeper lending relationships, and the higher flexibility with collateral compared to that demanded by formal rural financial intermediaries. Nevertheless, there are also risks associated with informal intermediaries, since they have poorer capital levels and higher market power. As a consequence, even if transactions costs are lower, they usually charge higher interest rates. Semi-formal intermediaries, such as credit unions, village banks, and cooperatives also enjoy some informational advantages in this environment.

Exclusion and financial development

Since financial underdevelopment and financial exclusion are strongly related in developing countries, it is convenient to analyse the importance of differences between developed and developing countries. Moreover, this analysis can also provide information as to the links between financial development and economic growth in developing countries. However, at this point, it should be noted that the relationship between finance and growth may be different depending on the state of economic development itself. In particular, there is much debate as to whether financial development fosters economic growth or if this relationship is the other way around. What is the direction of causality? Is it the same in developed and developing economies? There have been several initiatives – particularly from institutions such as the World Bank, International Monetary Fund (IMF) and the OECD – trying to disentangle the relevance of financial system development to economic growth in industrialised and developed countries. This section summarises this literature and aims:

- To show the dimension of the problem of financial underdevelopment in developing countries compared to industrialised countries. The main aim is to analyse evidence on financial penetration and the finance-growth nexus across countries; and
- To demonstrate that financial development is not necessarily pro-rich but also pro-poor, hence promoting financial inclusion.

Financial underdevelopment and the finance-growth nexus

Over recent years, there have been several studies that have assessed the degree of financial development and its impact on economic growth on a cross-country basis. Most of these studies have analysed financial deepening and financial dependence processes and the distinction between both concepts is very important in order to show differences between developed and developing countries.

Financial deepening is the level of development and innovation of traditional and non-traditional financial services. Most of the international studies employ a bank credit variable. King and Levine (1993) find a positive and significant correlation between bank credit development and faster economic growth and also a positive influence of financial liberalisation on bank efficiency reducing intermediation costs. Similarly, Rousseau and Wachtel (1998) suggest that financial development enhances long-run economic growth in early stages of industrial development. Rioja and Valev (2004) also find a positive relationship between financial development and growth although its significance is found to be different depending on the starting level of financial development. In developing countries, financial deepening is frequently associated with financial liberalisation processes.

Even if liberalisation increases financial flows in these countries, however, it does not guarantee larger financial penetration. Financial penetration is a measure of the degree to which savings are channelled through the financial system to provide financing for investment. Financial deepening and financial penetration are often employed indistinctly, while penetration is not always assured and liberalisation is not always efficient. These differences explain, for instance, why informal mechanisms – such as ROSCA's – survive in developing countries even if more formal microfinance programmes are also developing rapidly. Many individuals, for instance, will not be even willing to undertake any kind of formal business and they prefer to rely on informal lenders to obtain funds for their consumption needs (Fry, 1995, ch. 6).

Financial dependence is related to the extent to which households and firms rely on bank finance to undertake their investment projects. Therefore, financial dependence is particularly relevant in developing economies considering that households and firms in these countries rely heavily on (formal or informal) intermediaries. As for bank deepening, legal and institutional factors may also contribute substantially to explain the growth effects of financial dependence according to recent studies. Recent liberalisation of bank activities (with a trend towards broad banking in most financial systems) has been shown to increase financial intermediation efficiency and enhance their contribution to economic growth.[2]

Most cross-country studies have employed a variable of private bank credit (relative to GDP) to proxy the level of financial deepening and penetration in these countries. Even if this is a rough measure of financial penetration, these variables are employed – as noted by Fry (1995, p. 130) simply because of the lack of other data. Figure 8.1 show differences in financial development for a sample of industrialised and low- and middle-income countries employing the variable 'private credit of financial institutions to GDP' between 1990 and 2001. Two main conclusions can be drawn from this graph. First of all, although most developing countries have increased their level of financial (bank) penetration over the 1990s, they still significantly lag behind industrialised economies. It should be noted, however, that fast-growing Asian economies (such as Malaysia, Singapore and Thailand) have substantially increased their financial development in recent years. Secondly, some industrialised countries exhibit a reduction in the level of this variable. However, this does not necessarily mean a lower financial development but an increase in the participation of capital markets relative to banks in the financial system.

---

[2] See for instance: Arestis and Demetriades (1997); Jayaratne and Strahan (1996); La Porta *et al*, (1998 and 2002) or Carbó and Rodríguez (2004).

Figure 8.1   Private credit of financial institutions to GDP

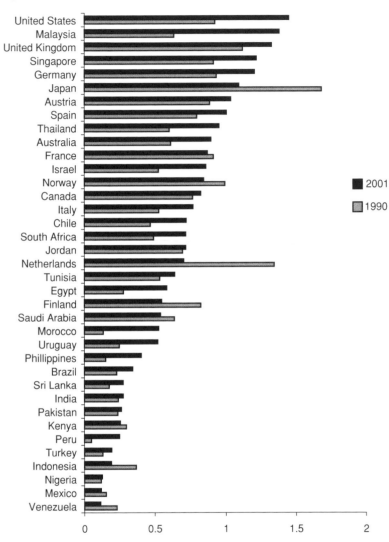

Source: World Bank Financial Structure Database[3] and own elaboration

---

[3] The World Bank Financial Structure Database is available at:
http://www.worldbank.org/research/projects/finstructure/database.htm

A study by Peachey and Roe (2004) uses a variety of financial deepening measures to evaluate access to finance in developing countries.[4] The study finds that:

- Sub-Saharan Africa is a long way behind other regions in terms of expanding access to financial services (and much of this is a reflection of the extreme levels of poverty seen in there);
- Asian economies are relatively advanced due to the rapid growth of the industrial base across most countries;
- The more advanced transition economies of Central Europe have seen substantial development in access to financial services since the 'huge' declines of the early 1990's, although CIS (Commonwealth of Independent States) countries lag far behind;
- Central and South American countries appear to have made little progress in extending access to financial services despite their relatively strong economic bases. This is especially the case for the large economies of Brazil, Argentina and Mexico.

Regarding the relationship between finance and growth, most of the recent studies have also shown that, no matter how we measure financial development, there seems to be cross-country association between financial system development and economic growth.[5] Analyses such as Levine *et al* (2000) have clearly demonstrated this type of association on a long-run basis, as shown in Figure 8.2.

However, it has also been pointed out that association does not imply causality. The important question is whether financial development causes economic development, or is it the other way around? The direction of causality is not trivial, and it is particularly important when analysing the role of finance in developing countries. Most of the theoretical models have relied on McKinnon-Shaw[6] type models. Fry (1995, pp. 20–38) surveys some of these models and relates them to liberalisation practices. The most important political implication is that economic growth can be increased by abolishing institutional interest rate ceilings and ensuring that the financial system operates

---

[4] See also Kempson *et al* (2004) for an interesting study on policy level response to financial exclusion in developed economies: lessons for developing countries.

[5] See World Bank (2001) for a comprehensive review of finance and growth literature and issues from a perspective.

[6] McKinnon (1969) and Shaw (1973).

Figure 8.2   Association between private credit and economic growth (1960–1995)

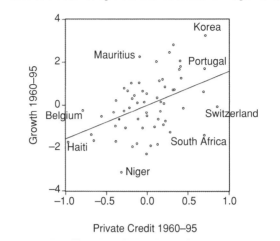

Private Credit 1960–95

Source: Levine *et al* (2000) p. 48

competitively under conditions of free entry. Interestingly, some studies such as Greenwood and Jovanovic (1990) have suggested a double direction of causality across a time horizon. In their model, economic growth favours the consolidation of a financial system in its early stages of development while a mature and consolidated financial system enhances more efficient investment decisions and faster economic growth.

As shown by Bencivenga and Smith (1991), the contribution of banks to growth in these causality relationships rely on their screening and monitoring functions that permit an easier, more efficient and faster access to external finance and increase the productivity of investments by reducing the holdings of liquid funds by households and directing them to illiquid but high-performance projects. Additionally, King and Levine (1993) demonstrated that changes in intermediation margins affect the growth rate of aggregate output and, interestingly, these changes are associated with the costs of financial innovation. Innovation increases efficiency and reduces risk, so that monitoring costs decrease and investment productivity increases for any given equilibrium growth rate.

Does financial deepening and financial dependence contributed to a reduction in financial costs in industrialised and developing countries? In order to compare the evolution of both types of countries, it appears to be convenient to express interest rates in real terms so that inflation

Figure 8.3   Real interest rates in industrialised and developing countries (percentage, medians)

Source: Honohan (2001) and own elaboration

differentials do not alter the evolution of rates over time. Figure 8.3 shows the medians – for periods of five year – of the money market, treasury bill and bank deposits rates in industrialised and developing countries employing the data provided by Honohan (2001). Interestingly, the figure shows that the comparatively lower real interest rate levels in developing countries during the 1970s and the 1980s were followed by higher levels during the 1990s. This is mainly due to a significant increase in inflation rates in developing countries that made it difficult for financial markets and intermediaries to develop in these economies.

Financial development is pro-poor

According to World Bank estimates (World Bank, 2001) a doubling of the ratio of private credit is associated with an average long-term growth rate almost 2 percentage points higher. These levels may be even higher in the case of developing countries. It is important to note that these estimations – as in most of econometric studies – already control for institutional and socio-economic infrastructure variables. However, there is also a concern about the relative impact of financial development in developed and developing countries. Is finance pro-poor or pro-rich? There are two main issues to be analysed in this context. The first is the impact itself of financial development in aggregate economic growth in developing countries. The second issue relates to the extent to which financial development improves or worsens income inequality within these countries. We wonder if there is a trade-off between financial development and income distribution.

The limited empirical evidence appears to favour the pro-poor view of financial development. Li, Squire, and Zou (1998) analyse data on inequality in 49 countries. Their results suggest that financial development reduces inequality in most of these countries. In particular, different measures of financial development are positively related with the poorest groups of the population distribution. Moreover, the relationship between income distribution and economic growth seems to be independent of growth or inequality levels, showing that financial development can improve income distribution as a higher proportion of population access financial services, reducing not only the number of poor people but also the income differences. In any event, further research is needed both within and across countries on these issues.

There is also empirical evidence that financial development poses a risk-reduction function. As long as the range of financial instruments and financial services innovations increase, it has been shown that aggregate economic volatility diminishes. In particular, Easterly, Islam and Stiglitz (2001) undertook a study on 60 countries, showing that the level of financial development is significantly and negatively related with output growth volatility. A doubling of private credit from 20 per cent of GDP to 40 per cent is predicted to reduce the standard deviation of growth from four to three per cent per annum.

Nevertheless, there are also risks associated with financial development, although most of theses are motivated by inefficient implementation of the necessary structural reforms. The main risk is associated with inflation. It is well-known that inflationary shocks associated with strong financial developments in the economy may increase output volatility in low- and middle-income countries. Therefore, if credit expansion is not accompanied by structural changes in the economic and the financial architecture of developing countries, financial development can be even harmful in the long term.

It is worth noting that the success of financial development reforms will depend on the appropriate development of institutional factors over the long-term – as relevant property rights and contract enforcement laws take a while to introduce. In addition, it takes time to reform financial systems so that the specific role of various financial intermediaries are clearly defined. Demirgüç-Kunt and Maksimovic (1998) analyse the relevance of legal and institutional environments on long-run growth rates employing a microeconomic sample of firms from 30 countries. Their results suggest that, if institutional factors are appropriately studied and controlled for, financial development is associated with wider access to external finance. Cetorelli and Gambera (2002) also study the role of external finance on economic growth. Their results suggest that the existence of regional financial intermediaries is particularly relevant to finance growth in bank-dependent financial systems. Even higher bank market concentration is found to be beneficial for bank credit-dependent industrial sectors and to improve credit conditions for junior firms entering the market.

As shown by Wurgler (2000), the role of financial deepening in financially less-developed economies, is not just to increase savings and financial flows but to mobilise resources to the sectors where they are needed. A positive mechanism is, therefore, the mobilisation of – though not necessarily an increase in – savings, the reallocation of investable funds, and increased reliance on external providers of finance.

Overall, although financial development has been found to foster growth, there are differences in the lessons learned for industrialised countries and low- and middle-income countries. Some of these lessons have been recently summarised by the World Bank[7]:

– First of all, increasing domestic credit at a very fast pace results in high inflation rates and depreciation problems. Macroeconomic stabilisation mechanisms are then of particular relevance here, since inflation and depreciation may also carry institutional insolvencies; and
– The creation of state-owned banks is not the best way of promoting the creation of financial development since it forces and politically alters the allocation of financial services and the proliferation of financial intermediaries within a country.
– Excessive protection of the financial services industry can lead to excess costs and poor services. Policy actions should be oriented to provide solutions to the financial requirements of households and

---

[7] See World Bank (2001) report, Chapters 3 and 4.

firms, as has been the case of the progressively more complex economic environments in developed countries.

Overall, policy actions in developing countries should aim to respond to their specific market needs and not to the particular needs of individual market participants. Therefore, governments need to promote the development of relevant 'architectures' for the financial system. The aim should be to provide infrastructure and institutional coverage that enables financial system participants to deliver the services in which they specialise with maximum effectiveness. At this point, it is also worth noting that there should not be an ex-ante preference for market-based against bank-based systems. Such a process should be encouraged when financial intermediaries have been shown to play an important role in providing finance to private agents in developing countries and, specifically, in rural areas. Each stage of the financial development process will require different policy actions that foster market and intermediary growth and the policy ingredients will depend on a proper analysis of market needs over time.

Mechanisms of financial inclusion in developing countries: informal financial networks and microfinance

Due to macroeconomic instability and the various institutional problems discussed above, formal financial intermediaries are faced by many obstacles to enter and expand their business in developing countries. Informal financial mechanisms have represented the main alternative to formal finance for a long time. However, in recent years, formal microfinance schemes have developed to become a major alternative for many households and firms (co-existing with informal lenders) as the main sources of finance in these countries. In this section, we provide an overview of informal financial networks and microfinance in developing countries, including some examples of recent experiences in various countries. Interactions between informal networks and microcredit programmes are also discussed since recent studies have suggested that microfinance does not reach the poorest of the poor (including those that do not even intend to undertake any business).

Rotating Saving and Credit Associations (ROSCA's)

Establishing a network of financial institutions in developing countries and, in particular, in rural areas, is expensive due to the absence of the proper institutional and legal infrastructures (as well as macro-economic instability). As such, formal intermediaries do not usually have adequate training, monitoring, and incentive structures so as to be encouraged to develop rural micro-credit and deposit-taking business. Consequently, informal finance has become an important source of finance for certain groups in almost all regions of the developing world.

In most of the developing countries, there are informal financial agents such as moneylenders, pawnbrokers, trade-related services and tied credit facilities. However, probably the most important informal networks are non-intermediated multilateral financial arrangements and, in particular, the Rotating Saving and Credit Associations (ROSCA's). As noted earlier in this chapter, a ROSCA is a savings club that is managed by their members by pooling regular savings and lending the pooled sum out in turn to the members. This way, these savings clubs can reduce the average time taken for a member to access a target investable sum. The success of this type of informal network can be explained by two main reasons: they are relatively easy to create and they are very transparent. No outsiders are involved, no one is beholden to anyone else, and no one can profit from anyone else's difficulties. Moreover, no money has to be stored by the managers of the ROSCA, because all cash passes from member to member directly.

In the presence of information problems and difficult risk management schemes, informal finance is a substitute that provides a range of alternative incentives and information devices, including social enforcement or social collateral, where possession and use of the assets offered as collateral is transferred to the lender. However, informal finance is not a perfect substitute for formal finance: Formal intermediaries exhibit a higher ability to mobilise funds on a large scale and pool risks over extensive areas.

Informal finance can only solve information problems related to financial relationships on a small-scale and for isolated customers. However, even in the cases where informal lenders – mainly ROSCA's – reach a relatively large operating-scale in pooling risk in villages, the volatility of individual household consumption is still far from being fully isolated from idiosyncratic household risk. The absence of adequate screening and monitoring schemes usually results in the choice of low-risk and low-yielding production processes.

The case of informal finance in rural China and India, for instance, illustrates some of these advantages and disadvantages. Tsai (2004) has recently undertaken a study on the role of informal finance in rural

China and India, with the aim of analysing the success and persistence of informal financial networks relative to new formal instruments such as micro-credit. Even if there has been a clear expansion of rural financial institutions in both China and India over the last several decades, informal finance still represents a major source of credit for many households and small firms and traders. In China, estimates from the International Fund for Agricultural Development (IFAD), reveal that farmers obtain four times more credit from the informal 'curb' market than from formal financial institutions. Financial regulators have also repeated efforts to eliminate and/or regulate 'curb' market activity. India has a longer history of state-directed credit for poverty alleviation. This country presents a more liberalised formal financial sector. However, these regulatory initiatives have not impeded the growth of a well-developed informal financial sector that usually takes similar corporate forms to ROSCA's.

Why, then, has informal finance persisted and even expanded in both countries over time? Tsai (2004) offers various explanations. Firstly, formal financial institutions and microfinance programmes are often unable to meet the demand for grassroots credit. Secondly, even if the supply of official credit were sufficient, the credit officers often face local pressures and incentives for credit distribution that deviate from the original intentions of state authorities of diminishing informal networks. Moreover, in many rural areas of India, the establishment of a village bank has even enabled pawnbrokers to expand their role as financial intermediaries to local populations. Similarly, the case of China has demonstrated that formal sector credit is more expensive to low quality borrowers than informal credit.

The microfinance revolution

Over the last three decades, we have witnessed a tremendous growth of microfinance institutions in developing countries. Microfinance is a key issue to reduce financial exclusion. The concept of microfinance itself has evolved rapidly over the years. At the beginning – with the first experiences in Bangladesh and Brazil in the late 1980s – microfinance represented a way of providing very poor families with small loans (micro-credits) to help them engage in productive activities or develop small businesses. Over the years, microfinance schemes have become the main mechanism of formal finance in developing countries and they are being also progressively applied in industrialised countries. The range of services associated to microfinance has increased to include not only credit, but a savings, insurance, payment services or even equity.

Two main factors explain the success of microfinance institutions as mechanisms for poverty alleviation and financial inclusion in developing countries. First of all, these institutions have exhibited significantly low levels of loan delinquency, at least compared to many subsidised lending schemes implemented previously in some developing countries. Secondly, they have reached a broad scope of societal groups that were previously neglected, even by informal lenders. The success of microfinance has also been attributed to certain characteristics of these programmes that are similar to those of informal finance, such as the use of dynamic incentives using regular repayment schedules and follow-up loans or 'progressive lending', and the existence of a 'lighter' management structures that reduce intermediation costs and make these institutions more competitive. These characteristics also explain why these advantages are being imported to developed countries where certain social groups are financially excluded.

Although the amounts involved in microfinance contracts are not quantitatively significant compared to traditional bank lending, these programmes are important in terms of the number of beneficiary households. In this context, the World Bank (2001) has noted that it would be a mistake to consider microfinance programmes just profitable banking techniques that do not need to be subsidised by lending programmes whose target is the poor.

Anderson and Locker (2002) for instance have shown that micro-credit programmes can increase common pool resources and social capital and lower the costs of social actions, in particular in rural settings. One of the main policy concerns in developing microfinance programmes has been the effective distribution of resources to the areas where they have the greatest social impact. However, even these programmes have not always been successful in increasing financial inclusion for the poorest of the poor. Although microfinance can reduce the problems of information and costs for small-scale lending, they do not always solve the problems of the poorest borrowers in developing countries. Better information mechanisms to improve monitoring and to avoid duplicities with informal finance networks are needed. Studying two of the most well-known cases – the Grameen Bank of Bangladesh and the experience of Bolivia – may help explain some of the benefits of microfinance and the problems faced in providing financial services to the poorest of the poor.

The Grameen Bank

Can subsidised microfinance offer greater social returns than alternative uses of funds? The case of the Grameen Bank in Bangladesh represents an interesting case study to answer this question. Grameen Bank was created in 1976, when Professor Muhammad Yunus, Head of the Rural Economics Programme at the University of Chittagong launched an action research project to examine the possibility of designing a credit delivery system to provide banking services targeted at the rural poor. (Grameen means 'rural' or 'village' in Bangladeshi language). As of July, 2004, it had 3.7 million borrowers, 96 per cent of whom were women. With 1,267 branches, Grammen Bank provides services in 46,000 villages, covering more than 68 per cent of the total villages in Bangladesh. Figure 8.4 summarises the main operations of Grameen Bank.

The interesting feature of the credit granting process of Grameen Bank (among other things) is that it:

- Exclusively focuses on the poorest of the poor,
- Organises borrowers into small homogeneous groups – as such characteristics facilitate group solidarity as well as participatory interaction;
- Applies special loan conditions that are particularly suitable for the poor – such as: very small loans given without any collateral; loans repayable in weekly installments spread over a year; close supervision of credit by the group as well as the bank staff: and transparency in all bank transactions; and it
- Promotes a social development agenda.

The success of the Grameen Bank is widely cited (see Khandler [1998], Morduch [1999] or Amin *et al* [2003]) as been a major influence in the development of microfinance programmes throughout the world. Even if social benefits attributed to Grameen exceed their costs, it may still be that a shift to full cost-recovery could yield even greater social benefit. This main mechanism would operate via expanded scale. However, as shown by Morduch (1999) this implies that if microfinance initiatives are to grow then funding for such developments may have to rely on capital markets. In this case, microfinance programmes would need to charge higher interest rates to their customers in order to offer investors returns similar to less risky investment options. From a social perspective, rising interest rates are likely to

Figure 8.4   Grameen Bank's operations

The underlying premise of Grameen is that, in order to emerge from poverty and remove themselves from the clutches of usurers and middlemen, landless peasants need access to credit, without which they cannot be expected to launch their own enterprises, however small these may be. In defiance of the traditional rural banking postulate whereby 'no collateral (in this case, land) means no credit', the Grameen Bank experiment set out to prove – successfully – that lending to the poor is not an impossible proposition; on the contrary, it gives landless peasants the opportunity to purchase their own tools, equipment, or other necessary means of production and embark on income-generating ventures which will allow them escape from the vicious cycle of 'low income, low savings, low investment, low income'. In other words, the banker's confidence rests upon the will and capacity of the borrowers to succeed in their undertakings.

Grameen Bank operates as follows. A bank branch is set up with a branch manager and a number of centre managers and covers an area of about 15 to 22 villages. The manager and the workers start by visiting villages to familiarise themselves with the local milieu in which they will be operating and identify the prospective clientele, as well as explain the purpose, the functions, and the mode of operation of the bank to the local population. Groups of five prospective borrowers are formed; in the first stage, only two of them are eligible for, and receive, a loan. The group is observed for a month to see if the members are conforming to the rules of the bank. Only if the first two borrowers begin to repay the principal plus interest over a period of six weeks, do the other members of the group become eligible themselves for a loan. Because of these restrictions, there is substantial group pressure to keep individual records clear. In this sense, the collective responsibility of the group serves as the collateral on the loan.

Loans are small, but sufficient to finance the micro-enterprises undertaken by borrowers: rice-husking, machine repairing, purchase of rickshaws, buying of milk cows, goats, cloth, pottery etc. The interest rate on all loans is 16 per cent. The repayment rate on loans is currently – 95 per cent – due to group pressure and self-interest, as well as the motivation of borrowers.

Although mobilisation of savings is also being pursued alongside the lending activities of the Grameen Bank, most of the latter's loanable funds are increasingly obtained on commercial terms from the central bank, other financial institutions, the money market, and from bilateral and multilateral aid organisations.

Source: Adapted from Grameen Bank's website at: http://www.grameen-info.org

reduce the net returns of borrowers and put credit out of reach for some, worsening the problem of reaching to the poorest of the poor.

A note on the microfinance experience in Bolivia

Microfinance programmes have proliferated in South America over the last decade or so and Bolivia probably represents the main example of the success of such programmes. Navajas *et al* (2000) analysed the experience of five of these organisations in La Paz. Their main was to show the actual reach (depth) of these microfinance programmes in order to find out if they really alleviated poverty in the most deprived areas. However, their results show that most microfinance organisations are actually serving not the poorest but rather those near the poverty line. The poorest are less likely to be creditworthy and this prevents them from demanding loans. At the same time, urban lenders had more market penetration than the rural lenders among the poorest. The study finds that rural microfinance programmes do not appear to reduce inequality since typical rural borrowers are more likely to be among the poorest. Their results, the authors suggest, highlight the need for more inspection of the flood of funds budgeted in the name of access to loans for the poorest. If the programmes are not implemented effectively – and even if they aim to alleviate poverty – they can not reach the population they formerly intend. In any event, it has been shown that, even if these microfinance organisations do not reach many of the poorest, this problem is more than balanced by net gains that accrue to those near the poverty line.

Development of formal intermediaries: some policy lessons

Although informal financial networks are playing an important role in many developing countries, they are not a substitute for formal finance. And although microfinance programmes are having a positive contribution in most developing countries, financial deepening – and particularly, financial penetration – is not secured simply by promoting (and subsidising) microfinance. Many individuals in developing countries remain excluded from financial services simply because they do not even intend to start up a business and their borrowing reputation is quite low in the view of other formal intermediaries. Consequently, there are two main types of policy efforts that should be distinguished:

i. Government initiatives – including financial liberalisation and institutional reforms – should be oriented to undermine the barriers that impede a proper expansion of formal intermediaries in developing countries. Fry (1995, pp. 317–351) indicates various areas where structural reform and other improvements are needed in order to achieve greater financial penetration in developing countries:
   • Lifting restrictions on bank activities, providing a variety of financial institutions and intermediaries. The latter does not imply direct actions against informal lenders in the short-run,

since they are recognised to play a productive role in the development process;

- A legal framework ensuring the enforceability of financial contracts and the supervisory systems, thereby improving property rights and consumer protection schemes; and
- Providing macroeconomic stability, controlling inflation with monetary control and fiscal discipline. Without stability, regulatory initiatives can be inefficient and even harmful for financial development.

ii. The future development of standard formal intermediaries will partially depend on the current prevalence of microfinance groups. At this point, a definition of the interactions between microfinance activities and informal networks is needed in order to avoid duplicities and to make microfinance more efficient.[8]

As for the development of microfinance and its relationships with the activities of informal intermediaries, Jain and Mansuri (2003) have recently analysed some of the main problems. They observed that informal lenders appear to be thriving even in regions where microfinance is present. A first problem is related to repayment systems. Grameen Bank and similar microcredit schemes require borrowers to repay their loan in tightly structured installments (frequently weekly installment over a year, with the first installment due immediately). In the case of informal credit networks, the greater flexibility of their installment structure allows them to survive. Moreover, microfinance may even benefit the co-existence of informal lenders. Since borrowers using microfinance know that repayment must begin almost immediately after loan disbursement, they will need to access other sources of funds to finance installment repayments, and these funds are typically borrowed from an informal source. As long as this situation occurs, the displacement of informal credit as a policy objective might be incorrect since the focus should be on whether the credit needs of borrowers are served.

Secondly, microfinance and informal lending are not perfect substitutes. Amin *et al* (2004) reveal that vulnerability can also partially explain some of the problems in microfinance reaching the poor, particularly in rural areas. The poorest in society find it most difficult to insure against idiosyncratic risks. The forces that make some poor

---

8 See World Bank (2001), Chapter 2 for further discussion on the interactions between microfinance and informal networks in developing countries.

households vulnerable may also make them represent greater risks for micro-credit providers. This is the main reason why micro-credit programmes often find it difficult to provide finance to the most vulnerable and poorest members of society in developing countries.

Conclusions

This chapter provides an insight into a range of issues relating to financial exclusion in developing countries. It can be seen that many of the areas relating to financial exclusion in the developed world have similarities in the developing world – although in the latter exclusion is amplified in many cases by significantly underdeveloped financial institutions and systems. We also note the broad literature on financial sector development and growth that finds that a developed financial system can promote economic advancement although there is no guarantee that this will reduce inequality. Developing countries have substantially limited financial systems and institutions with large parts of the population (particularly in rural areas) having no access to mainstream financial services. Typically informal channels are the major source of finance to poorer members of society and we outline the role of ROSCA's and other microfinance initiatives in bridging the financing gap. There is evidence, however, that these complement other forms of (more costly) informal finance (such as from moneylenders/'curb' markets) and it also seems that even these do not meet the needs of the poorest of the poor. More still needs to be done to improve financial inclusion in the developing world. A greater role played by governments acting as mediators in encouraging bank-based initiatives and possibly some affirmative action is likely to be the most effective approach to expanding access to financial services in the developing world. Affirmative action could be targeted on (domestic and foreign) banks in large cities forcing them to lend to deprived areas and the urban poor. A similar scheme, perhaps, could also focus on rural areas. There is a need for wider development of low-cost no-frills accounts, greater use of technology in providing access to financial services and policy needs to directed to improving the 'banking habit'. Developing policy to encompass these sort of factors should at least go some way to improving access to financial services in the developing world.

9
Financial Exclusion – Areas for Further Study

Finally, this brief chapter explores some areas, in our opinion, that deserve further attention regarding the study of financial exclusion. It is clear that financial exclusion is rapidly emerging as a 'hot topic' in European banking and financial policy areas. At the same time, there is a real and marked paucity of comparative and other kinds of empirical research on this area. Much more work is needed if financial exclusion is to be tackled in a sustained way and if banks are to play strategically a pro-active and value-enhancing role in this process.

A fundamental problem in this area is the need for robust and comparable data related to financial exclusion. These data are needed across time and countries. Good research and appropriate policies will be constrained until these data become more available. This has to be a priority, a 'necessary condition' for a viable research agenda. At the same time, benchmark standards need to be developed, agreed and carefully monitored. It is only with these in place and fully understood that a more credible analysis of the impact of greater financial inclusion and associated welfare improvements can be evaluated.

The following lists areas of study that we believe should be encouraged if we are to obtain a better understanding of the nature and features of financial exclusion. It will also help policymakers and banks in forming strategies to deal with this problem. The suggestions run from the main findings outlined in this text and area as follows:

1. A basic economic question is whether and how much financial exclusion matters in a developmental context. What are the specific economic gains from improved financial inclusion? This is an important question if governments wish to explore free market solutions that require banks to bid for some kind of government-financed

franchise to help overcome financial exclusion. A sound methodology for estimating these gains needs to be explored;

2. A comparative, cross-country study (using a case study approach) of how a targeted sector/sub-sector of banks are responding strategically to financial exclusion in different developed and developing countries is also needed;

3. Complementary (to 2) a statistical study on how the strategic characteristics of banks (including proximity banks – those located closest to customers) 'explain' regional development in both developed and developing economies. Such a study might differentiate bank strategies by *inter alia* their approaches to financial exclusion or by different bank types – mutual versus private and state-owned. Statistical tests may then be set up to see how these differences help to 'explain' different kinds of bank performance and regional development. Related statistical testing may also relate bank financial strength (and other strategic characteristics) to financial inclusion issues;

4. A comparative, case study and cross-country study of the success of a particular kind(s) of products (e.g. by replicating and extending the Gothenburg [Table 7.1] methodology) and/or institutions (e.g. credit unions, savings banks) in overcoming financial exclusion;

5. A statistical examination of whether greater 'statistical noise' is a significant factor in credit scoring certain groups of 'marginal' customers, especially those in 'financially desertified' regions;

6. A complementary examination of whether the omission of 'relationship' and other 'contextual characteristics' of prospective borrowers from contemporary credit scoring produces discrimination in lending and the consequences to the bank of this phenomenon.

7. A comparative and simulation-based exercise on how particular bank products and risk-reduction/risk mitigation methods might be developed for 'more risky' groups of customers.

8. A cross-country survey of the success to date of a particular scheme (like provision of basic bank accounts) or various types of government policies in helping to overcome financial exclusion.

These are just a small sample of non-mutually exclusive research projects that are needed to help inform the debate as to how to tackle financial exclusion and to assess the effectiveness of current country initiatives in the area. The results from such studies should help governments and financial intermediaries in both the developed and developing world in formulating effective policy aimed at increasing access to financial services. Ultimately, this should help to promote economic progress as well as social and political inclusion.

References

Alexander, A. and J. Pollard (2000), 'Banks, grocers and the changing retailing of financial services in Britain', *Journal of Retailing and Consumer Services*, pp. 137–147.

Allessandrini, Pietro, Luca Papi and Alberto Zazzaro (2003), 'Banks, regions and development', *BNL Quarterly Review*, No. 224, March, pp. 23–55.

Al-Yousif, Yousif Khalifa (2002), 'Financial development and economic growth. Another look at the evidence from developing countries', *Review of Financial Economics*, 11, pp. 131–150.

Amin, S., A.S. Rai and G. Topa (2003), 'Does microcredit reach the poor and vulnerable? Evidence from northern Bangladesh', *Journal of Development Economics*, 70, pp. 59–82.

Anderloni, Luisa (2003), 'Il social banking in Italia: Un fenomeno da esplorore', Fundazione Giordano Dell'Amore (Vanese: Italy).

Anderson, C.L. and L. Locker (2002), 'Microcredit, social capital and common pool resources', *World Development*, 30, pp. 95–105.

Arestis, P. and P. Demetriades (1997), Financial development and economic growth, assessing the evidence. *The Economic Journal*, 108, pp. 783–799.

Argent, N.M. and F. Rolley (2000), 'Financial exclusion in rural and remote New South Wales, Australia: a geography of bank branch rationalisation, 1981–98', *Australian Geographical Studies*, July, 38(2), pp. 182–203.

Arnfield, Beatrice (2002), 'Credit unions, the alternative American banks', *Retail Banker*, 31 July.

Association of British Credit Unions Ltd (ABCUL) (1999), *How To Create A Sustainable Credit Union*, October (Manchester: ABCUL).

Association of British Insurers (1999), 'Response by the Association of British Insurers to the Financial Services Policy Action Team (Unpublished).

Avery, Robert B., Paul S. Colem and Glenn B. Canner (2004), 'Consumer credit scoring: do situational circumstances matter?', *BIS Working Papers* No. 146 (Basle: Bank for International Settlements).

Bank of England (2000a), *Finance for Small Firms: A Seventh Report*, January (London: Bank of England).

Bank of England (2000b), 'Finance for small businesses in deprived communities', November (London: Bank of England).

Bank of England (2002), *Finance for Small Firms: A Ninth Report* (London: HMSO).

Bencivenga, V.R. and B.D. Smith (1991), 'Financial intermediation and endogenous growth', *Review of Economic Studies*, 58, 195–209.

Berger, Allen, N., Iftekhar Hasan and Leora F. Klupper (2004), 'Further evidence on the link between finance and growth: an international analysis of community banking and economic performance', forthcoming in *Journal of Financial Services Research*, 2004.

Berger, Allen, N.W., Scott Frame and Nathan H. Miller (2002), 'Credit scoring and the availability, price and risk of small business credit', *Finance and Economics Discussion Series* (Washington, DC: Federal Reserve Board).

Boyce, G. (2000), 'Valuing customers and loyalty: the rhetoric of customer focus versus the reality of alienation and exclusion of (devalued) customers', *Critical Perspectives on Accounting*, 11, pp. 649–689.

Brewer, Mike, Alissa Goodman, Michael Myck, Jonathan Shaw and Andrew Shepherd (2003), *Poverty and Inequality in Britain: 2004* (London: Institute for Fiscal Studies).

Bridges, S. and R. Disney (1992), 'Access to credit and debt among low income families in the United Kingdom: an empirical analysis', *mimeo*, available at: http://www.Nottingham.ac.uk/economics/ExCEM/index.html.

British Bankers Association (BBA) (2000), 'Promoting financial inclusion – the work of the banking industry – April 2000', 1 April (London: BBA).

British Bankers Association (BBA) (2000), *Inclusion – The Work of the Banking Industry – April 2000* (London: BBA).

British Bankers Association (BBA) (2002), *Promoting Financial Inclusion* (London: BBA).

British Bankers Association (BBA) Press Release (2003), 'Steady growth in bank accounts', 23 December (London: BBA).

Broome, John (1989), 'Should social preferences be consistent?', *Economics and Philosophy*, 5. 1 April.

Carbó Valverde, S., Humphrey, D.B. and R. Lopez del Paso (2003), 'The Falling Share of Cash Payments in Spain', *Moneda y Crédito*, Vol. 217, pp. 167–190.

Carbó, S. and R. López del Paso (2002), 'La inclusión financiera: un paso cualitativo más', *Cuadernos de Información Económica*, No. 170, September–October 2002, pp. 79–90.

Carbó, S., F. Rodríguez and R. López del Paso (2000), 'Las cajas de ahorros: algo más que instituciones financieras', *Cuadernos de Información Económica*, No. 158, September/October 2000, pp. 65–76.

Carbó Valverde, S. and F. Rodríguez Fernández (2004), 'The finance-growth nexus: a regional perspective', forthcoming in *European Urban and Regional Studies*, 2004.

Caskey, J.P. (1997), 'Lower income American, higher cost financial services' (Madison: WI: Filene Research Institute).

Cetorelli, N. and M. Gambera (2002), 'Banking Market Structure, Financial Dependence and Growth, International Evidence from Industry Data', *The Journal of Finance*, 56, pp. 617–648.

Chakravarty, S.P. (2004a), 'Regional bank networks and social exclusion', April forthcoming in *Regional Studies*.

Chakravarty, S.P. (2004b), 'Asymmetric information and Rothschild/Stiglitz', Unpublished note, School for Business and Regional Development (Bangor: University of Wales, Bangor)

Collard, Sharon, Elaine Kempson and Nicola Dominy (2003), *Promoting Financial Inclusion: An Assessment of Initiatives Using a Community Select Committee Approach* (Bristol: The Policy Press).

Clarke, Charles (2004), 'Green shoots', *Financial World*, April.

Cruickshank, D. (2000), *Competition in UK Banking: a Report to the Chancellor of the Exchequer* (London: HMSO).

Demirgüç-Kunt, A. and V. Maksimovic (1998), 'Law, finance and firm growth', *Journal of Finance*, 53, pp. 2107–2137.

Donovan, N. and G. Palmer (1999), 'Meaningful choices: the policy options for financial exclusion' (London: New Policy Institute).

Doyle, Joseph J., Jose A. Lopez and Marc R. Saidenberg (1998), 'How effective is lifeline banking in assisting the "unbanked?"', *Current Issues in Economics*, Vol. 4, No. 6, June.

Drakeford, M. and D. Sachdev (2001), 'Financial exclusion and debt redemption' in *Initial Social Policy*, Vol. 21(2), pp. 209–230.

Dymski, G. and W. Li (2002), 'The macrostructure of financial exclusion: mainstream ethnic and fringe banks in money space', *Rights to the City Conference*, May.

Easterly, W., R. Islam and J.E. Stiglitz (2001), 'Shaken and Stirred: Explaining Growth Volatility,' in Bruno Pleskovic and Joseph Stiglitz (eds), *Annual Bank Conference on Development Economics*, 2000 (Washington D.C.: World Bank).

Economic Research Europe Ltd (1997), *The Single Market Review: Impact on Credit Institutions and Banking* (London: Kogan Page).

ESRC Centre for Business Research, Cambridge (2000), *British Enterprise in Transition 1994–1999* (University of Cambridge: ESRC Centre for Business Research).

European Commission (2001), *Access to Financial Services – Strategies Towards Equitable Provision* (Brussels: EC Health and Consumer Protection Directorate-General).

Fry, M.J. (1995), *Money, Interest and Banking in Economic Development* (London: The Johns Hopkins University Press).

FSA (Financial Services Authority) (2000), 'In or out? Financial exclusion: a literature and research review' (London: FSA).

FSA (2000a), 'A cycle of disadvantage?: Financial exclusion in childhood', November (London: FSA).

FSA (2003) 'No Bank Account? – Why it could pay you to have one', May (London: FSA)

Fuller, D. (1998), 'Credit union development: financial inclusion and exclusion', *Geoforum*, Vol. 29(2), pp. 145–157.

Fuller, D. and A.E.G. Jonas (2002), 'Institutionalising future geographies of financial inclusion: national legitimacy versus local autonomy in the Britain credit union movement', *Antipode*, pp. 85–110.

Gardener, Edward P.M., Philip Molyneux and Jonathan Williams (2003), 'Competitive banking in the EU and Euroland', Chapter 5 in Andrew W. Mullineux and Victor Murinde (eds) (2003), *Handbook of International Banking* (Cheltenham: Edward Elgar).

Gardener, E.P.M., P. Molyneux and B. Moore (eds) (2002), *Banking in the New Europe: The Impact of the Single European Market Programme and EMU on the European Banking Sector* (Basingstoke, UK: Macmillan).

Geddes, M. and A. Root (2000), 'Social exclusion – new language, new challenges for local authorities', *Public Policy and Management*, Vol. 20(2), April–June, pp. 55–60.

Goodwin, Denise, Laura Adelman, Sue Middleton and Karl Ashworth (2001), 'Debt, money management and access to financial services: evidence from the 1999 PSE Survey of Britain, *Working Paper No. 8*, CRSP (Centre for Research in Social Policy).

Greenwood, J. and B. Jovanovic (1990), 'Financial development, growth and the distribution of income', *Journal of Political Economy*, 98, pp. 1076–1108.

Hayton, K. (2001), 'The role of Scottish credit unions in tackling financial exclusion', *Policy & Politics*, pp. 281–297 (Bristol: The Policy Press).

HM Treasury (1999), *Access to financial services*, PAT14 (London: HM Treasury).

HM Treasury (1999a), 'Credit unions of the future taskforce report', Press Release.

HM Treasury (1999b), *Enterprise and Social Exclusion*, PAT 3 (London: HM Treasury).

Hogarth, Jeanne M. and Kevin H. O'Donnell (1999), 'Banking relationships of lower income families and the Governmental trend toward electronic payment', *Federal Reserve Bulletin*, July.

Holden, P. and V. Prokopenko (2001), 'Financial development and poverty alleviation: issues and policy implications for developing and transition countries', Working Paper 01/160, *International Monetary Fund*. Washington D.C.

Honohan, P. (2001), 'How interest rates changed under liberalization: a statistical review' in Caprio, G. Honohan, P. and J. Stiglitz (eds), *Financial Liberalization: How Far, How Fast?* (Cambridge, U.K: Cambridge University Press).

Institut Für Finanzdienstleistungen e.v. (IFF), *Access to Financial Servies – Strategies Towards Equitable Provision* (Hamburg: IFF). Report to European Commission (2001).

Jain, S. and G. Mansuri (2003), 'A little at a time: the use of regularly scheduled repayments in microfinance programs', *Journal of Development Economics*, 72, pp. 253–279.

Jayaratne, J. and P.E. Strahan (1996), 'The finance-growth nexus, evidence from bank branch deregulation', *The Quarterly Journal of Economics*, 111, pp. 639–670.

Jones, P. (1998), *Towards Sustainable Credit Union Development* (Manchester: Association of British Credit Unions Ltd).

Jones, Rupert (1998), 'Credit unions to fill the banking gap for the poor', *The Guardian*, 29 July.

Joseph Rowntree Foundation (1995), *Inquiry into Income and Wealth* (York: Joseph Rowntree Foundation Findings).

Joseph Rowntree Foundation (1998), *Income and Wealth: The Latest Evidence* (York : Joseph Rowntree Foundation Findings).

Joseph Rowntree Foundation (1999), *Understanding and Combating Financial Exclusion*, March (York: Joseph Rowntree Foundation Findings).

Kempson, E. (1994), *Outside the banking system*, Rep. No. 6 Social Security Advisory Committee Research Paper (London: HMSO).

Kempson, Elaine and Claire Whyley (1999), *Kept Out or Opted Out?* (Bristol: The Policy Press).

Kempson, Elaine and Claire Whyley (1999a), 'Kept out or opted out? Understanding and combating financial exclusion' (Bristol, UK: The Policy Press).

Kempson, Elaine and Claire Whyley (1999b), 'Understanding and combating financial exclusion', *Insurance Trends*, 21, pp. 18–22.

Kempson, E. and T. Jones (2000), *Banking without branches* (London: British Bankers Association).

Kempson, Elaine, Edele Atkinson and Odille Pilley (2004), *Policy Level Response to Financial Exclusion in Developed Economies: Lessons for Developing Countries*,

The Personal Finance Research Centre University of Bristol, September 2004, Report commissioned by Financial Sector Team, Policy Division, Department for International Development (UK).

Khandker, S.R. (1998), *Fighting Poverty with Microcredit: Experience in Bangladesh*. Oxford University Press for the World Bank, New York.

Kim, Taeho (1993), *International Money and Banking* (London: Routledge).

King, R. and R. Levine (1993), 'Finance and growth, Schumpeter might be right', *The Quarterly Journal of Economics*, 108, pp. 717–737.

La Porta, R., F. López de Silanes, A. Schleifer and R. Vishny (1998), 'Law and finance', *Journal of Political Economy*, 106, 1133–1155.

La Porta, R., F. López de Silanes and A. Schleifer (2002), 'Government ownership of banks', *Journal of Finance* 57, pp. 265–301.

Leonelli, Lucia (2002), 'The posts: a full range of payment services', Chapter 4 in Ruozi and Anderloni (2002).

Levine, R. Loayza, N. and T. Beck (2000), 'Financial intermediation and growth, causality and causes', *Journal of Monetary Economics* 46, pp. 31–77.

Leyshon, A. and N. Thrift (1994), 'Access to financial services and financial infrastructure withdrawal: problems and policies', *Area*, 26, pp. 268–275.

Leyshon. A. and N. Thrift (1995), 'Geographies of financial exclusion: financial abandonment in Britain and the United States', *Transactions of the Institute of British Geographers, New Series*, 20, pp. 312–341.

Leyshon, Andrew, Nigel Thrift and Jonathan Pratt (1998), 'Reading financial services: texts, consumers, and financial literacy', *Environment and Planning D: Society and Space*, Vol. 16, pp. 29–55.

Li, Hongyi, Lyn Squire and Heng-fu Zou (1998), 'Explaining International and Intertemporal Variations in Income Inequality.' *Economic Journal*, 108, pp. 26–43.

Macfarlane, Richard, Karl Doyson and Bob Patterson (2002), *Community Development Finance Institutions: London Feasibility Study for London and Quadrant Housing Trust*, March (Salford: University of Salford, Community Finance Solutions).

Marshall, J.N., Willis, R., Raybould, S., Richardson, R. and Coombes, M. (1999), The contribution of British building societies to financial exclusion. London: Building Societies Association.

McKillop, D.G., J.C. Glass and C. Ferguson (2002), 'Investigating the cost performance of UK credit unions using radial and non-radial efficiency measures', *Journal of Banking and Finance*, 26, pp. 1563–1591.

McKinnon, R.I. (1969), *Money and Capital in Economic Development*. Brookings Institution, Washington DC.

Mills, James (2003), 'Call centres' rich list of customers, *Daily Mail*, October 20, p. 35.

Mishkin, Frederic S. (1997), *The Economics of Money, Banking and Financial Markets* (New York: Addison-Wesley).

Morduch, J. (1999), 'The role of subsidies in microfinance: Evidence from the Grameen Bank', *Journal of Development Economics*, 60, pp. 229–248.

Mullen, Ian (2001), 'Prosperity and morality: a partnership with Government' (London: British Bankers Association). Also featured in the *New Statesman*, 19 October 2001.

Mullen, Ian (2002), 'CFSI round table discussion on the Joint Money Laundering Steering Group', CFSI round table discussions at the City Club, London, 7 October.

National Consumer Council (1997), *In The Bank's Bad Books: How the Banking Code of Practice Works for Customers in Hardship*, December (London: National Consumer Council).

National Consumer Council (1999), *Consumer Concerns 1999: Consumers' views of advice and information on financial services*, A National Consumer Council Report of a Survey by the RSGB Omnibus Service (London: National Consumer Council).

National Credit Union Strategy Working Group (2001), *Unlocking the Potential: An Action Plan for the Credit Movement In Scotland* (Edinburgh: National Credit Union Strategy Working Group, Minister for Social Justice).

Navajas, S., M. Schreiner, R.L. Meyer and C. González Vega (2000), 'Microcredit and the Poorest of the Poor: Theory and Evidence from Bolivia', *World Development*, 28, pp. 333–346.

Northern Ireland Executive (1999), *The First New TSN Annual Report* (Belfast, Northern Ireland).

Office of Fair Trading (1999), *Left out in the Cold* (London: OFT).

Office of Fair Trading (1999), *Vulnerable Consumers and Financial Services: The Report of the Director General's Inquiry*, January (London: OFT).

Peachey, Stephen and Alan Roe (2004), *Access to Finance – A Study for the World Savings Banks Institute*, October (Oxford: Oxford Policy Management)

Pensions Commission (2004), *Pensions: Challenges and Choices, The First Report of the Pensions Commission* (London: HMSO)

Pollin, Jean-Paul and Angelo Riva (2002), 'Financial inclusion and the role of postal systems', Chapter 5 in Ruozi and Anderloni (2002, pp. 213–252).

Reifner, Udo, Ulrich Krüger, Jan Evers, Marco Habschick and Stefanie Jack (2000), 'Across to Financial Servies: German National Report for the 5th International Conference on Financial Services*, University of Gothenburg, 22–23 September.

Revell, Jack (1987), *Mergers and the Role of Large Banks*, Institute of European Finance Research Monographs in Banking and Finance, No. 2 (Bangor: Institute of European Finance).

Revell, Jack (1989), *The Future of Savings Banks: A Study of Spain and the Rest of Europe*, Institute of European Finance Research Monographs in Banking and Finance, No. 8 (Bangor: Institute of European Finance).

Revell, Jack (1991), *Changes in West European Public Banks and their Implications for Spain*, Institute of European Finance Research Monographs in Banking and Finance, No. 9 (Bangor: Institute of European Finance).

Rioja, F. and N. Valev (2004), 'Does one size fit all? A re-examination of the finance and growth relationship', *Journal of Development Economics* 74, pp. 429–447.

Rose, Peter S. (2002), *Commercial Bank Management* (New York: McGraw-Hill Irwin).

Rossiter, Jenny (ed.) (1997), 'Financial Exclusion: Can Mutuality Fill the Gap?' (London: New Policy Institute).

Rossiter, Jenny (ed.) (2001), 'Financial Exclusion: Can Mutuality Fill the Gap?' (London: New Policy Institute).

Rothschild, Michael and Joseph Stiglitz (1976), 'Equilibrium in competitive insurance markets: an essay on the economics of imperfect information', *The Quarterly Journal of Economics*, 90, 4, pp. 629–649.

Rousseau, P.L. and P. Wachtel (1998), 'Financial intermediation and economic performance, historical evidence from five industrialized countries'. *Journal of Money, Credit and Banking* 30, pp. 657–678

Rowlinson, Karen, Claire Whyley and Tracey Warren (1999), *Wealth In Britain: A Lifecycle Pespective* (London: Policy Studies Institute).

Royaly, Ben, Thomas Fisher and Ed Mago (1999), *Poverty, Social Exclusion and Microfinance in Britain* (Oxford: Oxfam and New Economics Foundation).

Ruozi, Roberto and Luisa Anderloni (eds) (2000), *Modernisation and Privatisation of Postal Systems in Europe: New Opportunities in the Area of Financial Services* (London: Springer).

Saunders, Anthony and Marcia Millon Cornett (2002), *Financial Institutions Management: A Risk Management Approach* (London: McGraw-Hill/Irwin).

Scottish Office (1999), *Social exclusion – opening the door to a better Scotland*, from website: Scottish Office, www.scotland-gov-uk/library/documents-w7/sima-00-htm.

Shaw, E.S. (1973), *Financial Deepening in Economic Development* (New York: Oxford University Press).

Sherraden, M. (1991), *Assets and the Poor: a New American Welfare Policy* (New York: M.E. Sharpe).

Sinclair, S.P. (2001), 'Financial Exclusion: an introductory survey' (Heriot Watt University, Scotland: Centre for Research into Socially Inclusive Services [CRISIS]).

Social Exclusion Unit (SEU) (1998), 'Bringing Britain together: a national strategy for neighbourhood renewal' (London: HM Cabinet Office).

Schuster, L. (2000) (ed.), *Shareholder Value Management in Banking* (Basingstoke, UK: Macmillan).

Tsai, K.S. (2004), 'Imperfect Substitutes: The local political economy of informal finance and microfinance in rural China and India', *World Development* 32, pp. 1487–1507.

The University of Salford (2001), 'Update on community finance solutions', Occasional Paper from the Forum for the Develoment of Community Based Financial Institutions, September (Salford: The University of Salford).

Thrift, N. and A. Leyshon (1997), 'Financial desertification' in J. Rossiter (ed.), *Financial Exclusion: Can Mutuality Fill the Gap* (London: New Policy Institute), pp. 11–16.

Trenor, Jill (1999), 'Eddie George urges big banks to tackle financial exclusion', *The Guardian*, 7 September.

Waite, N. (2001), *Welfare and the Consumer Society: New Opportunities for the Third way* (London: The Association of Friendly Societies).

Welsh Office (1999), *Building an Inclusive Wales* (Cardiff: Welsh Office).

Wenner, M.D. (2000), *Lessons Learned in Rural Finance: The Experience of the Inter-American Development Bank*, IDB Sustainable Development Department, Technical Paper Series, Washington.

World Bank (2001), *Finance for Growth: Policy Choices in a Volatile World*, Policy Research Report. (Washington DC: World Bank)

WSBI and World Bank (2004), *Access to Finance*, Conference sponsored by the World Savings Banks Institute and the World Bank, Brussels, 28–29 October.

Wurgler, Jeffrey (2000), 'Financial markets and the allocation of capital.' *Journal of Financial Economics* 58, pp. 187–214.

Index